Exploring Raspberry Pi 4

Learn how to create your projects with Raspberry Pi 4 and Scratch, Guide for New Users Programming Raspberry Pi 4 and Manual for Real Projects

Jason Casey

Disclaimer

The advice and strategies found within may not be suitable for every situation. This work is sold with the understanding that neither the author nor the publisher is held responsible for the results accrued from the advice in this book.

Table of Content

Table of Figures and Images

List of Tables

Introduction

Hey, congratulation on your purchasing a copy of the *Exploring Raspberry Pi 4: Learn how to create your projects with Raspberry Pi 4 and Scratch, Guide for New Users Programming Raspberry Pi 4 and Manual for Real Projects*. This book aims to expose you to the world of electronics engineering and computer science programming and where they interface.

Some people, including kids find learning to program a very tedious task, which is why many students run away from what they consider a geeky subject. The truth is, it doesn't always have to be like that. We can all learn to program, especially if it is introduced to us in a manner that we are already using, two without making assumptions about us knowing the basics. That way, we can begin to climb the ladder and make some progress with our learning process in a fun-filled way.

The Raspberry Pi was designed to solve all of that. It was designed to be a low-cost PC about the size of a credit card that students can set up on their own on the fly and use that opportunity to know about computer architecture in one fell swoop.

Since its introduction in 2012, the Raspberry Pi has gone ahead to be a computer of choice for many kids, hobbyists, project engineers, automation experts, engineers, and programmers. It has been a welcome bridge between the programming world and the physical world.

Most of this book is concerned with learning how to program the Raspberry Pi with Scratch. Scratch is a simple to use graphical-programming language that does not involve writing lines of codes.

This book is designed from a beginner's point of view, even for someone who has not had any previous experience with the Raspberry Pi or someone who has had previous experiences with earlier versions of Raspberry Pi but wants to make the foray into Raspberry Pi 4 and wants a different perspective on approaching the subject.

The book contains lots of projects that you can follow and a few exercises that you can play around with to increase your confidence. The book is practical, and it encourages readers to try out and experiment with everything they read because it believed that is the best way to practice and get better in this craft.

The language is simple to understand even though technicalities are not sacrificed.

We implore to take the plunge as you enter this exciting world of programming and electronics experience as you make the most out of this book.

Chapter 1

Let's Meet the Family of Raspberry Pi

 Raspberry Pi

When in 2006, Eben Upton and other co-founders of the UK charity, Raspberry Pi Foundation decided to create a small, affordable and very easy to learn computer programming systems that even kids could set up, configure and program, they had no idea that they were building a multi-billion dollar industry that had a lot of hungry hobbyists and specialist who wished for just the same thing as they had in mind. For Eben and friends, it was appalling that the study of Computer Science had been reduced to "How to Create Documents Using Microsoft Word" or "How to search for information on a Search Engine like Google." It seemed like nobody was learning to program anymore. The days when even daily languages were in codes, seem to have been abandoned and kids no longer wanted to create any physical toys for themselves.

Figure 1: A Typical Raspberry Pi Board

They hatched a plan that saw them creating what became known as Raspberry Pi, a type of electronic board that had all the components of a computer, including a processor, Ram, Ports, and CPU. This board was designed to be as small as your credit card. For many people who are used to bigger computers, it may be a little difficult for them to believe that a circuit board the size of a credit card will be able to do the job of a larger computer, especially in a demanding and data-hungry world that we live in. While that may be true in some ways that the Raspberry Pi is not the most powerful computer out there, it has been used to achieve a lot of powerful applications that even your everyday PC may not be able to achieve.

To make the Raspberry Pi easy to program, Eben Upton and friends decided to design the Raspberry pi to be able to use

4

a simple, powerful and computing scripting language called the Python. To make it even easier for kids or anyone not interested in writing text-based code, especially when they are just starting their programming journey, they designed it to also be able to work with another block-based programming language called the Scratch Program. And thus, at the end of their effort, the Raspberry Pi was born.

If you only recently joined the club of people who are proud owners of one of the 25 million Raspberry Pi's sold since the foundation started selling in 2012, or still wondering if this is something you want to do, then this should be a good time for you to take that plunge.

Figure 2: Kids Learning to Program a Robot with Raspberry Pi

The Raspberry Pi was not designed to replace your mainstream laptop or computer, even though it can do most of the things your PC does, the owners of Raspberry Pi designed it to be an affordable computer running on Linux operating system. Linux tends to be very popular among Engineers and hobbyist, probably because it is open source with most of the source codes available for tweaking and also because it is easy to configure it to do a lot more than the original owners may have designed the system to do, like in the case of Android, which has a based on the Unix operating system.

However, if you are just an average user who is not interested in the lines of codes that Engineers and hobbyist cherish but only interested in putting on your laptop and using your mouse to pick up programs on your screen, watching a movie, viewing pictures, editing your pictures, typing out documents, creating spreadsheet documents and even presentations, then the Linux version (or the more proper name distros) on which the Raspberry Pi runs is a very user friendly graphical interface like the more popular Windows 10 or your Macintosh operating system.

The Raspberry Pi has all the major parts that make up a computer and where it does not have a particular function on-board, it has provision for users to connect any other component that they consider important to them.

But beyond being a normal computer that people use in their everyday activity, the Raspberry Pi is instead very popular for many hobbyists who want to explore, monitor, control and interact with the environment around them.

So, unlike the regular PC that does not give you at out of the box ability to take input from the physical environment around you, the Raspberry Pi shines so well in this area that it is being used even in industrial applications, security systems, and automation processes.

The Raspberry Pi comes with a set of general-purpose input/output (GPIO) pins that can be used by the user to take inputs from physical components and send out outputs after analyzing those inputs. This has allowed people all over the world to be able to use Raspberry Pi as a platform to learn to program, improve on their programming skills, build physical products, create projects and explore the Internet of Things (IoT).

The aim of the Raspberry Pi Foundation has always been to reawaken the desire in people to be creative by making the entry point easy for anyone interested in scientific innovations without the hitherto high cost associated with the equipment required for such endeavors. This, it tries to do by providing high-performance computers to people at a rate that very many people can afford so that they can quickly settle down to learning, solving local problems and more importantly have fun doing what they love doing. The foundation goes out of its way to make a lot of free resources available to people who wish to learn how to compute, make things with computers, train educators and guide people who want to access digital and computing information.

The Raspbian, which is the open-source operating system of choice by the Raspberry Pi Foundation allows the Raspberry Pi to operate in the open-source ecosystem that the Linux operating system offers. As part of the open-source ecosystem, the Raspberry Pi Foundation also makes contributions to the Linux kernel by participating in various open-source projects and even sometimes releasing some of their open-source software.

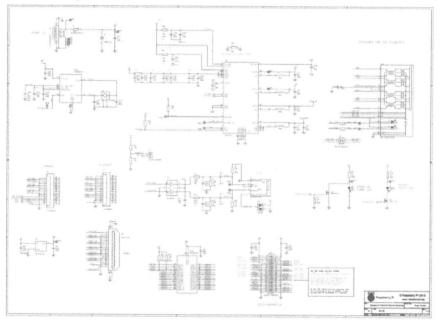

Figure 3: Raspberry Pi Schematics

The Raspberry Pi Foundation also promotes clubs like Code Club and CoderDojo by helping them grow their network around the world towards achieving their aim of having every child have access to learn about computing even though the programs do not have to be tied to the Raspberry Pi hardware.

That is not all, the Raspberry Pi Foundation also tries to organize events for enthusiasts of all ages to meet on the same platform to interact, learn and share ideas about projects and offer suggestions for solving issues. One such event is the Raspberry Jams.

Capabilities of Raspberry Pi (What you can do with it)

The Raspberry Pi is designed to be very small but mighty with a cost that is far lower than many video games yet suitable for learning how to code, build robots and create a wide range of fun and industrial projects.

It is capable of performing many of the functions that you may be used to performing on your computer, that include, but not limited to browsing the internet, playing games, listening to songs, watching movies and using the social media, even then the Raspberry Pi offers a lot more than a present-day computer.

The Raspberry Pi helps you to learn the inner workings of a computer, from assembling the system, connecting the respective hardware, and setting up your operating system yourself. It brings the two worlds of electronics and computer science together by helping learn how to connect the wires of circuits directly on the GPIO pins that are available on the board.

Depending on how you set it up, you can turn this small computer that is not even a super-fast computer into a processing device that can do everything from Christmas light, Robots, media servers, video game consoles, industrial and home automation system.

The different applications of the raspberry pi model are;

- Robotic Design
- Streaming Media Content
- Handheld Tablets
- Arcade machines
- Computers
- Home automation
- Online radios

Comparing Raspberry with other Boards

Although the Raspberry Pi is known to be very popular among computers and engineering enthusiasts, it is not the only available board available. Many alternative boards exist some of which are also aimed at hardware hackers, tech fanatics and software developers. Many of these boards are however not able to offer the same price, performance, and functionality that the Raspberry Pi offers. Examples of some of these boards include;

- La Frite
- NanoPi M4
- Odroid-H2
- Arduino

Some of these boards have their followers, but they tend not to be too many because of the compromise many of these boards have either in terms of video playback performance, video quality, number of ports, cost, Wi-Fi support or speed of the processor.

Generations of Raspberry Pi

As at the time of writing this book, the Raspberry Pi had been through four generations since inception that includes Raspberry Pi 1, Raspberry Pi 2, Raspberry Pi 3, and recently Raspberry Pi 4. Designed to be a go-to-computer for people of different ages and programming skills, each release of the Raspberry Pi comes in two variant models of A and B, with model A designed to be a cheaper variant with a smaller RAM, no Ethernet and a reduced number of USB ports.

The first time the Raspberry Pi was released was in February of 2012 and it was the Raspberry Pi 1 Model B. As expected, it has the least processing power, the smallest RAM and the fewest features among the main family of Raspberry Pi. It was the Raspberry Pi that opened the world to the possibility of what a small computer board about the size of a credit card could be used to achieve. It came with a price tag of $35, which is the same price that the Raspberry Pi foundation has always tried to maintain for all releases of the Raspberry Pi.

This was followed a year later by the cheaper Model A version. Then 2 years later, the improved designs of the Raspberry Pi 1 Model B+ and Model A+ were released.

In November 2015, the Raspberry Pi Zero was launched, it offered the cheapest and smallest package from the Raspberry Pi Foundation with its reduced number of ports, GPIO, and size. The Raspberry Pi Foundation Zero offered it as a minimalist alternative to the existing Raspberry Pi by sacrificing the standard GPIO, HDMI, Camera I/O, micro USB, and SD Card. This stripped-down version was sold at the cost of $5 per unit. Various versions of the Raspberry Pi Zero have also been introduced into the market at different times since then. The Raspberry Pi Zero W with Wi-Fi and Bluetooth capabilities is one such version and was released in February 2017 while the Raspberry Pi Zero WH which came with pre-soldered GPIO headers was released in 2018.

Next to be released in February of 2015 was the Raspberry Pi 2, which came with more RAM. After toiling with the idea of creating a strip down version of Raspberry Pi 1, the foundation came with what is described as the first significant upgrade to the Raspberry Pi 1 known as the Raspberry Pi 2 Model B. It offered a significant improvement in physical capacity, that included an increased number of USB ports, more SDRAM and a GPIO that had more strip.

At the software level, the Raspberry Pi 2 was even able to do video processing and handle more applications than its predecessor could handle. Compared to the Raspberry Pi 1 and the Raspberry Pi Zero, the Raspberry Pi 2 had a more spacious board that allowed for it to have a second set of USB ports. The Raspberry Pi 2 had one major drawback though, it did not have a Wi-Fi chip on board and instead relied on sacrificing one of the USB ports for users who connected a Wi-Fi dongle to be able to use it for wireless functions.

Next in line was the Raspberry Pi 3 Model B released in February of 2016. It came with a 1.2GHz, 64-bit quad-core ARM processor. The central processing unit (CPU) had a Broadcom system on a chip (SoC), Bluetooth, able to boot on USB and an on-chip graphics processing unit.

The Raspberry Pi 3 Model B+ followed after in 2018, it offered an increased processor speed of 1.4 GHz, embedded Wi-Fi and Bluetooth, Boot from USB, power over Ethernet (PoE) and an expanded network capability. The ability to boot from a USB was a very important feature because it meant that users now had the option to boot from a USB drive if they didn't want to use an SD card.

In June 2019, the Raspberry Foundation made a shock early announcement of the release of the Raspberry Pi 4 Model B. This model came with an increase in processor type and speed of 1.5 GHz, 64-bit quad-core ARM Cortex-A72 processor, embedded Wi-Fi, and Bluetooth 5 chips, full Gigabit Ethernet, two USB 3.0, two USB 2.0 and two ports for display (meaning you can display on two screens simultaneously). To get the most power from the system, users could buy the recommended power adapter from the manufacturers or ensure that they are using a compatible USB-C type port which allows the system to have more power to handle more peripherals. The Raspberry Pi 4 came in three onboard RAM sizes to choose from when ordering, the prices when released were; 1 GB ($35), 2 GB ($45), and 4 GB ($55).

Despite the release of the Raspberry Pi 4 model, it is expected that the production of the other models will continue. The production of Raspberry Pi 1 A+, Raspberry Pi 1 B+, Raspberry Pi 2 B, Raspberry Pi 3 B, and Pi Zero is expected to continue until at least 2022, while the Raspberry Pi 4 is expected to still be in production until at least 2026.

	Model (release date)	Price
1	Pi 1 Model B (2012)	$35
2	Pi 1 Model A (2013)	$25
3	Pi 1 Model B+ (2014)	$35
4	Pi 1 Model A+ (2014)	$20
5	Pi 2 Model B (2015)	$35
6	Pi Zero (2015)	$35
7	Pi 3 Model B (2016)	$35
8	Pi Zero W (2017)	$35
9	Pi 3 Model B+ (2018)	$35
10	Pi 3 Model A+ (2019)	$25
11	Pi 4 Model B (2019)	$35

Table 1: Generations of Various Raspberry Pi

Why Raspberry is Increasing in Popularity

Although the Raspberry Pi can be set up to be used as a normal PC, many people who buy the Raspberry Pi buy it to learn how to code and build electronic systems for their physical projects. The Raspberry Pi allows people who derive satisfaction in taking up electronic challenges, which makes it one of the reasons it is very popular with the hobbyist community.

Another reason why the Raspberry Pi is very popular is that it creates the opportunity for people to create their home automation projects without the need to use closed proprietary systems. Using a Raspberry Pi will allow you to exercise greater control over how your system will work.

The presence of Raspberry Pi GPIO of up to 40 pins also makes it very attractive to engineers and hobbyists. With the GPIO, you can connect various external devices like simple LED systems, servo motors, sensors, and motors. Raspberry Pi also has the option to get an add-on call Sense Hat that allows the user to take advantage of the accelerometer, gyroscope, magnetometer, thermometer and pressure sensor. There are very few boards that have the same functionality as the Raspberry Pi and still have those kinds of GPIO pins for interaction with the physical world. The number of things, you can make with the Raspberry Pi at home are enormous, you can create your arcade machine, light detection system, web server and anything your imagination can conjure up.

When it comes to access to accessories, there are very few products that have the level of information, support, library, online tools, add-on and accessories as the Raspberry Pi does, the various forums, subreddit, Instructable, and DIY subreddit.

For those who are already conversant with electronic systems, the Raspberry Pi is a fast board compared to many of its competitors. It also tends to have more RAM size than many of those competitors on a per size basis and usually comes with many USB ports with Ethernet, Bluetooth, and wireless capabilities.

The ability of Raspberry Pi to multitask and run as a normal computer with the Linux operating system is another reason why Raspberry Pi is popular among computer enthusiasts. By using the power of Linux, users can make the system perform a wide range of functions like the VPN server, media center, and print server.

Raspberry Pi also has a large, active community where users can go to and ask questions about issues bothering them. The community is available for students, teachers, hobbyists, and even hackers worldwide.

Understanding the Raspberry Pi Naming Convention

If you have read this book up to this point, you would have seen that the Raspberry Pi comes in different generations which can easily be identified by the naming convention used for each of them.

If you, however, just jumped to this part of the book, you may need to go to the section that talks about the different generations. In any case, the Raspberry Pi has a naming convention that has the letters A, B, and B+ that follow the models of the Pi except the Raspberry PI Zero and Raspberry Pi Compute.

If you've been looking into buying a Raspberry Pi, you may have noticed an unusual naming convention when naming Raspberry Pis. The letters A, B, and B+ follow most models of the Raspberry Pi (except the Pi Zero and Pi Compute) but what do they mean?

Knowing what they are for is very important to anyone who intends to study the Raspberry, they are used to refer to the type of board. When the board type is a 'B' board, it is used to signify the original Raspberry Pi, which is the size of a credit card. That means the first generation of Raspberry Pi will be called Raspberry Pi 1 Model B, ditto for the second generation of Raspberry Pi, which will be called Raspberry Pi 2 Model B, and Raspberry Pi 3 Model B for the third generation of Raspberry.

When the board type is an 'A' board, it is used to signify a smaller and squarer Raspberry Pi of the generation of that board. That means the first generation of the smaller and squarer Raspberry Pi will be called Raspberry Pi 1 Model A, ditto for the second generation of the smaller and squarer

Raspberry Pi, which will be called Raspberry Pi 2 Model A, and Raspberry Pi 3 Model A for the third generation of the smaller and squarer Raspberry Pi 3.

The Raspberry Pi Foundation also tends to a revised board to the B type board with the name B+. The name B+ is an indication of an improvement in the specification of the board type with certain features upgraded. So, we can have the Raspberry Pi 1 B+ as an improvement on the Raspberry Pi 1 B the same way the Raspberry Pi 3 B+ is an upgrade on the Raspberry Pi 3 B with improved specification and performance.

Despite the differences between these models, the Raspberry Foundation still tries to ensure the basic board only cost $35 no matter the generation of the Raspberry Pi.

Choosing a Raspberry Pi Type for your Projects

So, you have gotten to this point and want to give the Raspberry Pi a shot, but you are finding it difficult to make a choice.

Perhaps you need one as a teaching aid in your school, or for your kid or your home project or your industrial application, you could be confused about which of the models to buy. This can be particularly confusing if you are just a beginner and want to simply use the Raspberry Pi to enter the world of programming. Knowing what you want will allow you to resist the temptation of buying the cheapest board available or just buying the most expensive without having a justification for it.

The eleven Raspberry Pi models come in various CPU speeds, processor types, different RAM sizes, physical size, network connectivity and slots for expanding peripherals.

Your choice of a Raspberry Pi should be influenced by the demands of the proposed project, which means that your choice will be determined by your present requirements and the possibility of expansion. You may also want to ensure that the speed of the processor has the processing requirement of the system you are working on. You also want to consider the number of ports on the board, especially the USB port which could be influenced by what you want to use it for. Another consideration is if your application requires you to have a board with Bluetooth and wireless capability when making your choice.

The availability of the Raspberry board type in your local vicinity will also probably influence what boards you have access to. It may be easier to have access to some types of boards in some countries than it is to have in other board versions. This restriction is however no longer as pronounced with the use of eCommerce sites when placing orders. Many eCommerce sites now deliver worldwide.

As a rule of thumb, you can follow these simple guidelines:

If your project is meant to be a low-cost project where the networking capability is not a necessity or not required from a security point of view, then a Raspberry Pi Model A can be used.

For projects where cost is not the most important consideration, but instead, a powerful processor is a more important criterion, then the Raspberry Pi Model B will be suitable for your project even as a beginner.

For industrial applications, Raspberry Pi Compute should be your board of choice because of the many I/O lines it has. This model also has very good CPU capacities, making it suitable for applications in industrial settings.

The Raspberry Pi Zero is the model of choice for projects that are low budget, have space constraints but still require wireless onboard connectivity.

The beauty of the boards from Raspberry is that they will continue to be in production, which means that whatever specific device you require will most likely be available whenever you need them. That means if you identify a specific version of a Raspberry Pi board that meets your design needs, you are likely to have access to it whether it is the lower spec Raspberry Pi A+ family, low-cost Raspberry Pi Zero or the even the recently released Raspberry Pi 4.

However, if you intend to benefit from using this book, then I suggest that you go for the Raspberry Pi 4. The Raspberry Pi 4 comes as a powerful board with a price range from $35 to $55 depending on the size of RAM you want to buy.

Components of a Raspberry Pi Board

The Raspberry Pi Board is about the size of a credit card, if you physically hold the board, you may be tempted to wonder what a board of that size can do especially when you compare it with the size of either desktop or laptops. So, let us explore the different components you will find on a Raspberry Pi board.

On-board Chip

The most important part of the components that make up a Raspberry Pi board is the ARM CPU/GPU. This is the brain of the board and is referred to as System on a Chip (SoC). The processor has an ARM central processing unit (CPU) that handles all the processing, computations and information processing and a videocore4 GPU for the processing of graphical output.

The GPIO Pins

These are the pins that give the Raspberry Pi the connection point to be able to interact with the outside world. The physical extensions enable hobbyists to connect and tinker different transducers and components like LEDs, servo motors, controllers and even extension boards. If a hobbyist were to attempt to achieve the same thing with a normal laptop, he would have to start facing the challenges of getting the right adapter that will enable the person to connect with a USB port or serial port of the computer, after that, the person will then have to worry about having the right drivers and other serious configurations. With the GPIO on the Raspberry board, programmers can perform various operations on the GPIO pin using the computer program and control various devices even up to eight servos right out of the box without any additional hardware.

The SD Card slot

One way this small device can save some space is by not having an on-board hard disk as a normal laptop has, instead an SD card is used to play the role of a hard disk or solid-state drive (SSD). Recent boards use the microSD card slot which is where the SD card for the operating system (OS) required for booting the system is installed.

RCA Jacks

The RCA jack is used to connect and send videos to analog TVs and other RCA video devices. They are great for compatible devices or other similar output devices.

Audio Jack

This is useful for connecting your headset or speaker over a standard 3.55mm audio jack. There is no audio-in, but the board can accept Linux compatible mics.

Ethernet

Some variants of the Raspberry Pi boards (B Models) come with Ethernet ports with 10Base-T and 100 BaseTX Ethernet support that allows them to be used for wired network access.

USB Ports

These ports enable users to connect a lot of peripheral devices, including keyboards and mouse. This is one major area that the Raspberry Foundation takes into consideration when creating a stripped-down version of boards by reducing the number of ports.

The HDMI Port

The Raspberry Pi is equipped with a High Definition Multimedia Interface (HDMI) output port, which allows users to hook up to compatible televisions or monitors.

The Power Port

The power port is a 5V micro-USB power input connector like the power port of most tablets and mobile devices. There is no on-board power regulator on the Raspberry Pi so there is a need to ensure that the power input is within the regulated value.

Chapter 2

Introduction to Raspberry Pi 4

If you are not among the people who already own at least one of the 25 million Raspberry Pi boards that have been sold, then you could not have come in at a better time as the Raspberry Pi 4 board will be an amazing entry point for you.

The Raspberry Pi 4 is a massive advancement to its predecessors with new features that address some of the concerns the previously released boards had. Coming at a time no one expected it, the Raspberry Pi 4 model broke away from the tradition of having Raspberry Pi boards released in February or in the winter months to be announced in June of 2019 instead.

The device comes with various upgraded hardware specifications that many users will find interesting. It comes with a Broadcom BCM2711, Quad-core Cortex-A72 (ARM v8) 64-bit SoC with a processor speed of up to 1.5GHz, support for 4k display, two USB 2.0 ports, two hyper-fast USB 3.0 ports, Bluetooth and wireless capabilities, and a Gigabit Ethernet connectivity.

This new version 4 takes the Raspberry Pi family to a whole new level, which makes it able to handle projects that require more power, provides amazing features including better graphics and quality videos that make it suitable for it to be used as an entertainment hub and gaming console. It also has two micro-HDMI ports that make it able to display on two monitors of output up to 4k video. When the display is split across two output devices, it can do two 4K displays at 30Hz and a single 4K display at 60Hz. At a fraction of the cost, this device can rival very powerful laptops and desktop PCs.

Perhaps one of the most important things to note about the Raspberry Pi 4 is that it is the first of the different versions of the releases of the Raspberry Foundation to come with different RAM sizes. With a starting price of $35 as prior models for a 1GB, users can immediately get a device that is two to four times faster than its predecessors. Other variants of the Raspberry Pi 4 introduced include the 2GB and 4GB of RAM, which is the largest Raspberry Pi ever released and four times more than the previous highest

RAM value. For beginners who are making an entry into the Raspberry Pi world, this is a powerful device to be starting with and can even be used as a budget desktop PC for someone searching for a PC of less than $100. If the Raspberry Pi 3 B+ was a decent desktop PC, the Raspberry Pi 4 can offer a far more decent performance that can even surpass the value of other laptops that cost a lot more than its price.

With a Raspberry Pi 4 board, you are now able to create simple and complex systems. You can make robotic arms, home automation, Wi-Fi enabled CCTV system, full security architecture, standalone web server, drone control units, media center, and industrial applications. You can even use it to create a personal retro gaming system, that has the traditional arcade joystick and buttons.

Although as with other Raspberry Pi, the storage is again handled with the SD card, the inclusion of the USB 3.0 offers the device a faster port for anyone who wants to hook up a fast SSD storage.

With the number of features the Raspberry Pi 4 has, it not only surpasses the manufacturer's goal of using the Raspberry Pi to provide a way for kids to learn how computer systems, hardware, and software work using a low-cost computer, but it also provides a capable device for experienced developers to use as an inexpensive computer. The Raspberry Pi 4 offers a highly compelling all-round performance, software application, and stability that makes it a device of choice for tech enthusiasts interested in designing various applications even as beginners.

Raspberry Pi 4 Specification

The Raspberry Pi 4 deviates from the previous versions of the Raspberry Pi and typically comes with a power adapter made specifically for it using the new USB-C power connector which allows devices to receive access to an additional 500mA. The USB-C connector provides support for OTG, which allows for connecting the Pi directly to the PC's USB port enabling it to be possible to locally access the device. The USB-C is a high bandwidth, reversible, symmetrical connector with a smaller and more durable size than the more popular USB-A. It is the only connector that can handle the Thunderbolt™ 3 and power devices of up to 100W. As you advance in the Raspberry Pi world, you will begin appreciating the exciting features of being able to use the USB-C in connecting high-speed USB devices.

The preceding models of the Raspberry Pi had their onboard Ethernet LAN port on the USB hub, which had an impact on the speed of the port. For the Raspberry Pi 4, the Ethernet port is a fully dedicated Gigabyte with superior speed. The board boast of a new 1.5GHz, 64-bit quad-core ARM Cortex-A72 CPU (ARM v8) processor that sits on a BCM2837 SoC (System on Chip). This processor allows the board to be able to support its 4k video output and the prospects of offering stunning HD videos for projects that involve media streaming.

The release of the Raspberry Pi 4 also ushers in the Raspbian Buster, which is based on the Debian 10 Buster. Buster has an improved user experience on the desktop interface that comes with the Chromium 74 browser, the new Mesa V3D video driver. These features make it able to run 3D applications on the desktop.

Buying the Raspberry Pi 4 model comes with an improved system specification. Here's what you should expect when you decide to buy it:

- 1.5GHz, 64-bit quad-core ARM Cortex-A72 CPU (ARM v8, BCM2837)
- 1GB, 2GB, or 4GB RAM (LPDDR4)
- On-board wireless LAN (dual-band 802.11 b/g/n/ac)
- On-board Bluetooth 5.0, low-energy (BLE)
- 2 qty of USB 3.0 ports
- 2 qty of USB 2.0 ports
- 40-pin GPIO header
- H.264 (1080p60 decode, 1080p30 encode)
- Gigabit Ethernet
- Micro-SD card slot
- OpenGL ES, 3.0 graphics
- USB-C power
- Combined 3.5mm analog audio and composite video jack

- Power-over-Ethernet (this will require a PoE HAT)
- H.265 (4Kp60 decode)
- CSI camera port
- DSI display port
- 2 qty of micro-HDMI ports (up to 4Kp60 supported)

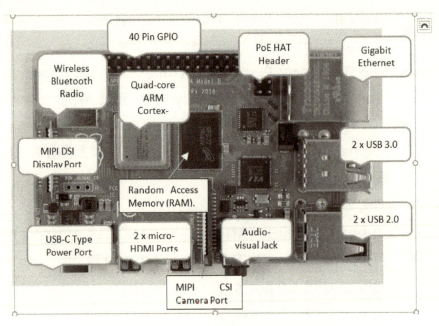

Figure 4: Components of the Raspberry Pi 4

Raspberry Pi 4 Accessories' Backward Compatibilities

If you are one of those who have already purchased one of the over 25 million Raspberry Pi boards already sold, you may be wondering if you can employ your previous Raspberry Pi accessories with the new Raspberry Pi 4 to save money on accessories since it seems they have the same credit card-sized boards.

Fortunately, in most cases, the new Raspberry Pi model B board makes use of the same types of accessories. However, as we have already seen, the B model comes with a new power connector which means that there may be a need for the person to buy a new adaptor for the Raspberry Pi model 4, one thing you will not need to consider upgrading on your Raspberry Pi 4 is the MicroSD card.

If you intend to reuse your case or considering getting a new case, you will have to pay attention to ensure you are acquiring the appropriate one for a Raspberry Pi 4 because of the new micro-HDMI ports, USB-C power connectors and new arrangement which has slighter altered the form of the Raspberry Pi board compared to the previous ones.

The new Raspberry Pi Raspbian Buster which is the operating system of choice for the Raspberry Pi 4 still has some difficulty integrating with some software at the moment. The Raspbian Buster Python libraries require some updates to make them compatible with the new OS.

Those in the gaming world may want to be sure they can do without the popular gaming emulator software, Retropie as it is not yet officially supported by the Raspberry Pi 4, although there is presently a workaround it for those skilled enough to do it. At the moment, another emulation platform, Kludge is the software supported by Raspbian

Buster. You may also opt to download Lakka even though it is still in its beta stage.

If an arcade machine is very important to you and you wanted to use the Raspberry Pi 4 to build one, it is important to confirm you can integrate it with this Raspberry Pi version before buying, otherwise, an older model like the Raspberry Pi 3 B+ may be your best bet.

Exploring the Raspberry Pi 4 Board

If you are buying a computer today, you would expect to find that the inner components of the computer will be housed inside a housing frame with just the display, ports, input devices available for the user to work with. However, with the Raspberry Pi, it is a different ball game because it comes with just the raw board. You, however, have the option to develop or buy a case for it if you want to enjoy enhanced protection for it and make it look a lot more presentable, otherwise, you could use the board the way it is and nonetheless have the functionality of a PC for your use. This is one of the significant things that makes the Raspberry Pi a great learning tool for teachers, students, and developers around the world.

Figure 5: Using a Raspberry Pi without a Case

By learning to plug various components and peripherals into the different ports, beginners can learn more about the computer. If you are holding a Raspberry Pi while reading this section of this book, it is essential to orient it to align with what is showing on the images used throughout this to be able to follow the description. This is particularly important when dealing with the pins on the GPIO header.

A Raspberry Pi 4 may look like an over-packed board considering its size, the board becomes less overwhelming as soon as you get used to the components, the role each of them plays and their inner workings.

Every PC, mobile phone or computing device will always have a CPU on it, whether you can identify it or not. For the Raspberry Pi 4, it is the component with the silvered colored metallic cap, the system-on-chip (SoC) beside the black integrated circuit (IC). This processor represents the part of the board that handles all the data and information flow of the whole system. The SoC also houses the Graphics Processing Unit (GPU) of the board which is the part that handles the visual aspect of the system.

We briefly mentioned the black IC beside the SoC in the section above, well, that is the Raspberry Pi 4's Random Access Memory (RAM). The RAM represents the part of the system that handles all the activities that the Pi is performing at any point when working with it. It stores all data being processed as long as the system is powered, but as soon as the system loses its power, it loses all its content which is while it is referred to as volatile memory. For any data you want to keep having access to including the next time you switch on the system or want to access on a different system, you will need to store that information in a non-volatile memory like the MicroSD card, USB stick or external hard drive.

Still on the board, you will see another metallic, silvered colored component. This used to have the Raspberry Pi logo engraved on it, on the Pi 3, apparently, this is not the case with the Pi 4. This is used to cover the radio, which represents the component of the board that gives the Raspberry Pi its wireless connectivity functionality. The radio has the Wi-Fi and the Bluetooth radio component.

Furthermore, on the board at the back of the USB port is another black IC with VLI written on it, that serves as the network and a USB controller. It is responsible for handling the data exchange between USB devices and networks.

Just behind the USB-C port which serves as the power button, is another IC is known as the power management integrated circuit (PMIC) used for managing the power from the power adapter on the Pi 4 board. It manages the power demands of the different peripherals connected to the board.

Away from the board ICs, let's move to the more conspicuous less technical parts of the board. The first of those will the Universal Serial Bus (USB), many people throw the name USB around without really knowing the meaning of the abbreviation, well, not so for you any longer. The Raspberry Pi 4 comes with 4 USB ports, two of which are the USB 3.0 and the other two are the USB 2.0. If you are confused about how to differentiate the two types of USB, then know that the USB 3.0 has the blue plane inside it, whereas the USB 2.0 has the grey plane color within it, it should be pretty easy to differentiate.

On the other side of the USB 3.0 is the Ethernet port which is also known as the network port for connecting the Raspberry Pi to a wired computer network using an RJ45 connector through an Ethernet cable from a modem. The Ethernet port equally has two light-emitting diodes (LED) at the bottom that serve as the status LEDs signaling to you that the connection is working when it is blinking.

Just beside the USB-C port used for powering the board are two similar ports. These are the two micro High Definition Multimedia Interface (micro-HDMI) port. The two micro-

HDMI allows the board to be projected on two different displays at the same time. You can connect one output to your TV and the other to your computer monitor.

Next to the two micro-HDMI ports is the 3.5 mm audio-visual (AV) jack. This is similar to the kind of jack you will find on most devices that allow you to plug in a headphone. Even though this port is commonly used as a headphone jack, not many people realize the port can also be used to transfer the video signal which can be connected to projectors, TVs, and displays that support composite video signals by using a Tip Ring Ring Sleeve (TRRS) adapter which is a special type of cable dedicated to that purpose.

Between the AV jack and the micro-HDMI is a connector that has a plastic flap that can be pulled up and used for connections in place. It has "camera" written beside it and is known as the Camera Serial Interface (CSI). It is the port into which the Raspberry Pi special Camera Module can be plugged into.

On the other side of the board is another connector identical to the camera connector, with display written beside it, it is the Display Serial Interface (DSI) or display connector designed to be used in connecting Raspberry Pi Touch screen displays.

Now back to where the Ethernet port is, you will notice a set of pins split into two rows. The pins are 40 in number in two rows of 20 each and are known as the GPIO (general purpose input/ output) header of the Raspberry Pi. It is this

35

component that gives the Raspberry Pi an advantage over the traditional PC or laptop because it allows the Raspberry Pi to speak to other hardware like the LED, buttons, robots, sensors and other external hardware devices in a way a Laptop would be unable to. It is the part used to collect data and send commands to various devices connected to the Raspberry Pi.

Just adjacent to the GPIO is another header called the Power over Ethernet (PoE) HAT. This small header contains just 4 pins and can be used to power the Raspberry Pi from a network connection rather than the micro USB socket.

Next, there is another vital port on the Raspberry Pi, the MicroSD port which is where the MicroSD card is inserted for loading the operating system, installing the software and the operating system that runs the Raspberry Pi.

Raspberry PI 4 Model B

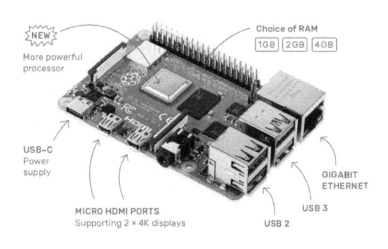

Figure 6: Layout of the Raspberry Pi 4

Comparing Raspberry 3 with Raspberry 4

Raspberry Pi 4 contains a faster processor than the processor for Raspberry Pi 3B+.

The Pi 4 takes advantage of the advancement in USB technology by introducing the USB 3.0 to this new board while reducing the number of USB 2.0 ports on the Pi 3.

The Pi 4 does away with the micro USB power port formerly been used for the USB-C port.

Another difference between the Pi 4 and Pi 3 is that the Pi 4 comes with two micro-HDMI ports compared to the single full-sized HDMI port available on the Pi 3.

The Pi now uses a new Raspbian variant which improves on the security, technical improvements, and updated applications compared to the Raspbian used by Pi 3. The Pi 4 also provides support for OpenGL 3.0 Graphics which the Pi 3 does not do.

The decision to change the position of the Ethernet port by exchanging its position with some of the USB ports on the Pi 4 also makes it sometimes not compatible with some Pi 3 enclosure or cases even though they have a similar form factor measuring 85.6mm × 56.5mm, however the Pi 3 and Pi 4 provide similar GPIO compatibility with Pi Hats.

The Pi 4 has a current requirement of a minimum of 3A compared to the 2.5A that the Pi 3B+ requires. For a project that has a low energy demand, the Pi 4 may not be the best option instead the Pi A Raspberry family may be more suitable. This can be a critical consideration when designing projects for remote locations that require low energy consumption and small batteries. The power adapter of the Pi 4 requires 15W to function properly.

The Pi 4 has the same Wi-Fi speed, on both the 5GHz and Pi 4 relies on a quad-core 1.5GHz Arm Cortex-A72 based processor on the new BCM2711 system-on-a-chip (SoC) while Pi 3 B+ uses a quad-core 1.4GHz Arm Cortex-A53 CPU on the older BCM 2837 SoC.

The memory on the Pi 4 has the options of 1, 2 or 4GB of LPDDR4 memory while the Pi 3 has just 1GB of LPDDR2 memory option.

Although both Pi 3 and Pi 4 have the Gigabit Ethernet, the speed of the Raspberry Pi 4 is still faster than that of Pi 3 which has a maximum throughput of 300Mbps because of its reliance on the USB 2.0 bridge.

2.4GHz as the Pi 3.

Specification	Raspberry Pi 4	Raspberry Pi 3
Processor	Broadcom BCM2711, Quad-core Cortex-A72 (ARM v8) 64-bit SoC @ 1.5 GHz	Broadcom BCM2837B0, Cortex-A53 (ARMv8) 64-bit SoC @ 1.4GHz
Memory	1GB, 2GB, or 4GB LPDDR4-2400 SDRAM (depends on model)	1GB LPDDR2 SDRAM
Connectivity	2.4GHz and 5.0 GHz IEEE 802.11ac wireless, Bluetooth 5.0, BLD	2.4GHz and 5GHz IEEE 802.11 b/g/n/ac wireless LAN, Bluetooth 4.2, BLE
	Gigabit Ethernet	Gigabit Ethernet over USB 2.0 (max throughput of 300Mbps)
	2 USB 3.0 ports; 2 USB 2.0 ports	4 USB 2.0 ports
Video and Sound	2 micro-HDMI ports (up to 4kp60 supported)	1 full-size HDMI port
	2-lane MIPI DSI display port	DSI display port
	2-lane MIPI CSI camera port	CSI camera port
	4-pole stereo audio and composite video port	4-pole stereo audio and composite video port
	Micro-SD card slot for loading OS and data storage	Micro-SD card slot for loading OS and data storage

Multimedia	H.265 (4Kp60 decode)	No 4K support
	H.264 (1080p60 decode, 1080p30 encode)	H.264, MPEG-4 decode (1080p30); H.264 encode (1080p30)
	OpenGL ES, 3.0 graphics	OpenGL ES 1.1, 2.0 graphics
Input Power	5V DC via USB-C connector (minimum 3A)	5V/2.5A DC via micro USB connector
	5V DC via GPIO header (minimum 3A)	5V DC via GPIO header
	PoE-enabled (requires separate PoE HAT)	PoE-enabled (requires separate PoE HAT)
Production Lifetime	At least until January 2026	At least until January 2023

Table 2: Between Raspberry Pi 3 and Raspberry Pi 4

The GPIO header on the Raspberry Pi 4's makes it able to support other connections like the UART, I2C, and SPI interfaces by using four more pins and a clock stretching support over I2C interfaces.

If you are fortunate to have a 4k display, the Pi 4 provides support for 4k displays with its crystal-clear images.

Chapter 3

Setting Up the Hardware

The Raspberry Pi 4 is designed to be remarkably quick and easy to set up and install for immediate usage and like any other computer, it relies heavily on other external components.

A Raspberry Pi 4 on its own represent just a board and can do nothing, it has to work with other components to become fully functional. For starters, it will require a MicroSD card for storing data, a display like a monitor, LCD or TV to visualize what you are executing, a 5V power source and input devices like the keyboard and mouse. Since many of us are already used to purchasing a finished encased system, you may be tempted to think that setting up a Raspberry Pi by starting with a bare board may be a complex process, but this book will try and make the process of setting up your system an easy one.

The Raspberry Foundation has also released a list of official accessories to be used with the Pi 4 and if you are buying a starter kit, the following items are what you may have delivered to you.

Raspberry Pi 4's Start-up Kit

Raspberry Pi 4 Power supply

The Raspberry Pi 4 uses a USB-C port for connecting its power supply, but the first edition of the Pi 4 tends not to work with some USB-C cable types which is why it is recommended that you order the starter kit that comes with a Raspberry Pi 4 charger.

Figure 7: USB-C Type Power Cable

This power supply will be better able to cope with the rapid switching power demands associated with the Pi 4. The charger comes with the spec;

41

Input: 100-240V ~ 50/60Hz 0.5A

Output: 5.1V --- 3.0A, 15W

Raspberry Pi 4 Enclosure or Case

The Raspberry Pi 4 can undoubtedly be used as it is without a case as long as you do not place it on a surface that conducts like on a metallic can that can cause a short-circuit. The pi case provides an extra layer of protection against static electricity, protects against bending pins and makes it easier to carry around. The enclosure that comes with the Raspberry Pi 4 already has the port positions marked out and in place so that it is easy to start it up immediately after purchase.

Figure 8: Official Raspberry Pi 4 Case

Raspberry Pi 4 Heat Sink

When you use a case for your Pi 4, it is important to know it can get hot during usage, which can make the covered board overheat, the starter kit therefore also will include a heatsink to help to conduct that heat away. The official enclosure equally has no slot for where you can put a fan, so if you believe your project will place a lot of demand on the Pi 4 which will result in a lot of heat being generated, be prepared to drill the required holes for your fan to use. Many unofficial cases have places for a fan to be installed, so do bear that in mind.

Figure 9: Heat Sink for Processor

Micro-HDMI cable

Another very important part of the starter kit is the micro-HDMI cable. If you only have the regular HDMI cable lying around in the house, it is better not to be caught by surprise and find you are not able to use the board when it arrives. The micro-HDMI cable will ensure you can connect your Raspberry Pi 4 to at least one display, do not forget that the Pi can connect to 2 display devices at the same time.

Figure 10: Micro to HDMI Cable

MicroSD Card

Another item that comes with the Raspberry Pi 4 starter kit is a MicroSD card that possesses the appropriate version of the Pi 4's NOOBS operating system already installed. This is likely to be tremendously useful to beginners who want to bypass the fascinating process of downloading the operating system and rather get to exploring the system right out of the box. With this approach, once you insert the MicroSD card in the right slot and have all the cables connected, you merely have to start up the system, boot it into NOOBs, select the Raspbian distribution and sit back while it installs.

Figure 11: Micro SD Card

Auxiliary Hardware and Kits to Get More from Raspberry Pi 4

Raspberry Pi 4 Desktop Kit: Full desktop computer kit

This is similar to buying a very cheap computer that comes with a 4GB Ram, a mouse, power supply, a guidebook, two micro-HDMI cables, a 32GB MicroSD card already loaded with NOOBs, and a keyboard. All you need to do is just to hook it up to an HDMI display or display(s) if you plan to use more than one display.

This is ideal for people who just want to acquire a uniformed colored system from the same supplier working, right out of the box and very suitable for people just getting started with Raspberry and the Linux software. The Raspberry keyboard comes with the Raspberry logo in place of the windows or Apple Logo you will find on those other keyboards.

Naturally, you don't need to buy the Pi 4 Desktop Kit when you already have all these peripherals. The mouse, external storage, keyboard, and Micro HDMI, that you may already have are equally able to work with the Pi 4.

If you are opting for desktop use of the Raspberry Pi 4, the 4GB RAM should your board of choice because as you will find, it is a bargain for its price. Pi 4 provides an affordable way for anyone who makes a cheap and fun Linux desktop, to be able to create a media center, plex server or a low power NAS.

Third-party Accessories

As expected, the Raspberry Pi 4 just like its predecessors is compatible with many other third-party applications and hardware which has opened a market for makers of any product conceivable to make use of the system.

Figure 12: Raspberry Pi 4 Case Produced by Third-Party Manufacturer

One More Thing, You Require a Working PC

This is not a part of the peripheral to connect, but it is necessary to include a working PC with internet access for you to format the MicroSD card, download the initial setup software for your Raspberry Pi and extract the files into the MicroSD card. This process will be explained in the next step and not necessary if you are using the full desktop kit from Raspberry.

You will also need to have a way to connect the MicroSD card to the PC using an adapter.

Chapter 4

Raspberry Pi 4 Operating Systems

Before setting up the hardware and connect all the peripheral, you have to prepare the MicroSD card it is time to set up its software which includes the operating system, the base software that administers what the Pi can do.

The default operating system (OS) designed for the Raspberry Pi is Linux. That can be frightening for some people, who still consider the Linux OS too techy for them, but there is really nothing to worry about. Linux has grown from its early days where it was just a black screen with a series of codes running through the system to be a system that presently has a graphical user interface just like your

Windows 10 or your Mac. It presently comes in various flavors or distributions all designed to make regular users who merely want to start operating the computer without understanding what happens under the hood operate the computer easily as they have now come to be used to with the experience of using Windows and Mac PCs. The Raspberry Pi 4 uses Raspbian buster as the operating system based on the Debian version of Linux and an upgrade on the Raspbian version used by Pi 4's predecessors.

By now you would know the Pi is not designed to have a hard disk so to install the operating system, you must download and copy an image of the disk into a MicroSD card, the same card we have been talking about all this while. It is the installation image that the Pi will use in booting.

The New Out Of Box Software (NOOBS) operating system is the installation manager that beginners and even experts can use in managing the installation process of the operating system for the Raspberry Pi 4. When you use the NOOBS in installing the operating system for the Raspberry Pi 4, it will allow the user to select from any of the operating systems in the standard distributions. MicroSD cards that come from any of the official Raspberry global distributors, resellers and Raspberry Pi site, or alternatively, if you get your MicroSD card from other sources, you can

download   NOOBS   from
The Raspberry Pi Foundation provides the Raspbian operating system for users to download and install alongside other third-party operating systems that include Windows 10 IoT Core, Ubuntu, specialized distribution for Kodi media center and RISC OS. Although Pi 4 has support for many programming languages, the Raspberry Pi Foundation, however, promotes the use of Scratch and Python software because of the ease of these programming languages compared to some other difficult system out there, which makes it suitable for the foundation to affect their target audience of young kids and people who have little or no programming skills.

Set Up the MicroSD Card

Download the SD Formatter

To prepare the MicroSD card for use, you will need to first format the card to a form that the Pi 4 can read. Please note that formatting the SD card will wipe out whatever previous data was on the card, so if the MicroSD card contains anything valuable to you, now is a good time to copy it somewhere and back it up. With that out of the way, you can now proceed to format the MicroSD card.

To format the MicroSD card for use with a Raspberry pi, you have to first visit the SD Association's website and download the SD formatter for your Windows or Mac PC. You can download the formatter from the website https://www.sdcard.org/downloads/formatter_4/.

Figure 13: SD Memory Card Formatter Interface

Download the SD Memory Card Formatter for your system in a folder that you can easily locate on your computer When the download is completed, locate the folder where the file downloaded to begin the installation process

Install the Formatter

Begin the installation process by double-clicking on the downloaded file

Install the SD Memory Card Formatter using the default settings

Follow the process through to the end

Format the SD Card

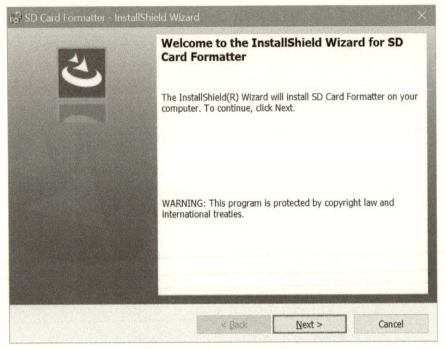

Figure 14: Installation of the SD Formatter

Startup the SD Memory Card Formatter and ensure the "Format Size Adjustment" option is set to on

Make sure you have the correct MicroSD card selected and click "Format" to format the card

Download NOOBS to your PC

With the MicroSD card formatted correctly, it is time to download NOOBS from the Raspberry Pi website, https://www.raspberrypi.org/downloads/noobs/.
Download to your desktop or to any folder you can easily access.

Extract NOOBS from Zip Archive

Next, you will need to extract the files from the zip archive containing the NOOBS files you downloaded from the Raspberry Pi web site. To do that, you will have to double click the download NOOBS zip file to open it.

Copy the Extracted files to the MicroSD Card

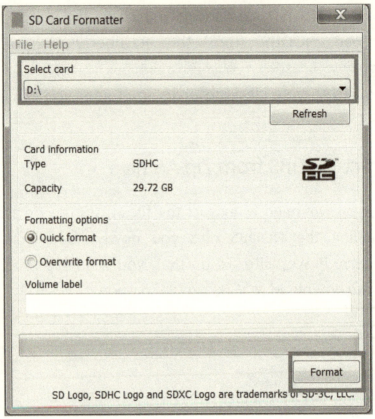

Now open another Window's Explorer or Mac's Finder window and navigate to the SD card and open it. Now select all the files in the extracted NOOBS folder that you opened in the previous step and drag them into the opened MicroSD card window to copy it inside.

Once the files have been successfully copied, you can eject the MicroSD card.

Chapter 5

Putting it Together

Now, you have the Raspberry Pi 4 board that you purchased, unpacked the box, have the NOOBS software on MicroSD card and want to get started. You have to now put it together so that you can start exploring the world of the Raspberry Pi ecosystem. To start, you will need to set up the whole system by connecting the different peripheral that makes up the hardware installation. The Raspberry is okay to use without a case provided you watch out for a short-circuit which can be avoided if you are using the optional Pi case or enclosure. It is equally best practice to consistently grip the board on the side by the edges rather than holding it on its flat side.

Now that you may have got your Raspberry Pi 4 and ready to get started. Now that you are familiar with the Pi 4, its specification and architecture, it is only logical that you should want to get down to business.

So even if you have little or no prior experience with computers, you can get right down to business if you just follow the instructions in the following steps.

Install the MicroSD Card

Before you undertake this step, you have to ensure that the MicroSD card already has the operating system on it, and this is likely to be the case if you bought the Pi 4 starter kit, but if you bought just the Pi 4 board and got the SD card from another source, it will be suggested that you use a minimum of 8GB, although 16Gb or 32Gb will be preferable. To install the MicroSD card into the Pi 4, you will have to identify the slot designated for it and slide the card into the slot with the label facing up.

The MicroSD card should be able to go in without you having to exert a lot of pressure. This card is used by the Raspberry Pi to boot from the operating system, store documents, load games, and other programs. A MicroSD card reader may also be necessary to connect the card to a PC.

If you were to ever want to extract the card in the future, you simply grip the end of the card and pull it out gently. If you ever find you have to force anything into or out of slots, then know you are doing something wrong.

Connect Keyboard and Mouse

This is quite straight forward, you simply plug the mouse and the keyboard into any of the available USB slots. Just ensure that the USB connectors are positioned correctly so that there will be no need to force it in.

Connect Display(s)

To connect the Pi 4 to a display, ensure you have the appropriate micro-HDMI to HDMI cable. You then connect the micro end of the board to the Pi 4, while the broader end of the micro-HDMI to HDMI cable is connected to the display. You will do the same if you are connecting more than one display to the Raspberry Pi 4.

If the only type of cable you have is the traditional HMDI cable, then you will have to get a micro-HDMI to HDMI adaptor. A standard PC monitor or TV can be used as long as it has at least one HDMI port for the connection. If the display has more than one HDMI port, then you have to identify the number indicated on that port and change the input type on the display to reflect the port number of the port you connected your Pi 4 to. If you are not quite sure, you can try changing the port number on the display until you get to the accurate one.

If on the other hand the monitor or TV does not have an HDMI port and you do not plan to invest in getting an HDMI display, then you can opt instead to get an HDMI to DVI-D,

HDMI to Display or HDMI to VGA adapter cables to convert the HDMI port into a suitable one for the type of display.

Connect Network Cable

If you plan on connecting your Pi 4 to a wired network, then you will need an Ethernet cable with an RJ45 connector on both ends. To connect it, you put the RJ45 into the Pi's Ethernet port. The plastic flip must be facing down as you push it in until you hear a click. Same way, the other end is connected to any free port on your network hub, router or switch. When you want to remove the Ethernet cable, you'll have to just press the flip-up plastic towards the plug and gently move the RJ45 connector out.

Figure 15: Final Set-Up of the System

Connect your Power Supply

The power port of the Pi 4 is similar to the USB-C used by many smartphones. If you plan to use the power supply adapter for a smartphone, you want to be sure it is the type that can deliver 15W power to accommodate the demands of the peripherals connected to the Raspberry Pi 4.

The Raspberry Pi does not have a power button to switch it on or off, so connecting the Raspberry Pi to a power supply marks the last step in the setting up of the hardware and only done when you are ready to set up its operating system because the Pi will turn on as soon as it is connected to a live power supply.

To connect the power adapter, face the micro end of the USB to the Pi board correctly. If you are using the official Raspberry Pi power supply, you will notice you will have different types of mains connectors of different countries for you to choose from. Just identify the one that matches the socket of your country and slide it into the socket as you would normally do.

Power your Device

When all is accomplished, you can take a deep breath, do a last-minute check to be sure you performed everything correctly. Once you are convinced everything is connected as it should be, then that is a good time to switch on the socket and power up the Raspberry Pi.

Chapter 6

Startup your Raspberry Pi

As we have already stated, the Raspberry Pi does not come with a power switch and will come on as soon as it is connected to a power outlet. A red LED light will come on, to indicate the Raspberry Pi is connected to its power source and is going through its booting process. During this booting process, pictures of raspberries will show up at the top left corner of the screen. This will take a couple of minutes before the next screen shows up.

When the Pi switches on or is booted for the first time with a fresh image of NOOBS on its MicroSD card, you will be greeted with a screen that displays the Raspberry Pi logo on it with a little progress window at the upper left part of the screen.

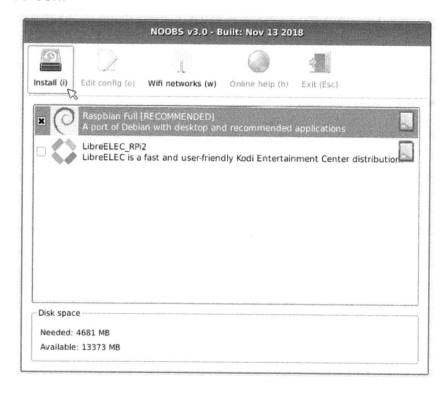

Figure 16: Select Raspbian for Installation

As soon as the installer gets loaded, you will be offered an opportunity to select from one of the standard operating systems that come standard with the NOOBS. Raspbian comes pre-installed with lots of useful educational, programming and productivity software that you can instantly start using when you start. It equally has Python, Scratch, Java, Sonic and many other programming languages.

Since you are just starting the system with NOOBS on your MicroSD card, the NOOBS installer will come up. It is easy to follow the installer which is also quite intuitive and will walk you through the Raspbian Operating System (OS) installation process. To make the installation a little less stressful, various features of the operating system will be displayed to you as the installation process happens underground.

Select the checkbox for "Raspbian Buster with desktop and recommended software" and click "Install" and "yes" to the warning in the dialogue box that shows up informing you that any data currently stored on the MicroSD card will be overwritten when installing the operating system and the installation process will start.

You can now go and grab a cup of coffee or a glass of water as the installation process continues. You can expect it to take some bit of time. The process bar will show you the status of the installation process. The time for the installation process can be anything between 10 and 30 minutes, which depends primarily on the speed of your MicroSD card and RAM size.

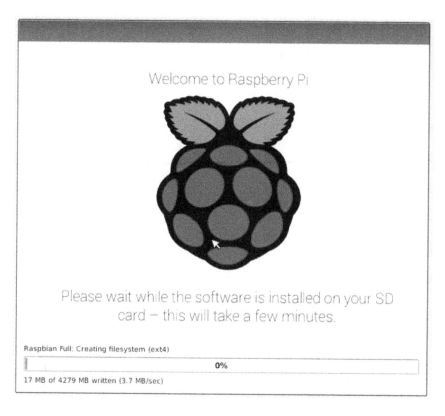

Figure 17: Installation Process of Raspbian OS

Booting it up for the First Time

When the Raspbian installation is completed, click "Ok" in the pop-up window and your Raspberry Pi will restart into the newly installed operating system and boot up your Raspbian desktop. Since this is the first time this is coming up, it could take a couple of minutes to optimize the operating system, manage the available space on the MicroSD card and adjust and set up the environment for the newly installed programs.

Finally, the Raspberry Pi logo will appear briefly before loading the Raspbian desktop with the wizard.

Figure 18: Completion of Installation

The booting process will get to a window where it will say "Welcome to the Raspberry Pi Desktop", not long after you will get to the Raspbian Desktop. At this stage, the installation process of your operating system is now complete and ready to be configured.

Setting up the Operating System on the Raspberry Pi 4

If Microsoft Windows or Apple macOS are the only types of computers you have ever used, you have nothing to worry about because the Raspbian OS has the same feel and uses icons, menus, mouse pointer, and desktop similar to what you are already familiar with in those other operating systems.

Setting up the Welcome Wizard

Figure 19: Welcome Screen during Installation

When you run the Raspbian for the first time, you will be greeted with the "Welcome to Raspberry Pi" wizard pop up to steer you through the configuration and setup process.

Begin by clicking the "Next" button, you will be prompted to select your country, set your language and select your time zone on the screen that comes up.

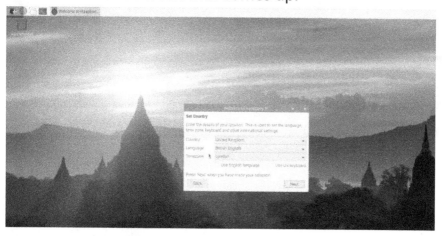

Figure 20: Selecting your Country

Subsequently, you click "Next", which will bring up a screen where you have the option to set a password for the system. There will be a message displayed in this window that informs you that the default password for the 'pi' user account is 'raspberry'. The message will also strongly recommend you change this to a different password known to you alone. You have the option to click the checkbox next to 'Hide Passwords' to toggle between showing the password you've chosen in the 'Enter new password' and 'Confirm new password' fields or not. The two passwords must be the same and if they are, you can click "Next" to move to the next stage.

Figure 21: Set New Password

If you have a wireless router, this next screen will prompt you to choose your Wi-Fi network from among the list of networks available. By the time you get to this stage, you should be armed with the network pre-shared key of the wireless router you want to connect to. So now, find and select your network name by clicking on it and then click

"Next". Enter the password which is the same as the pre-shared key we just talked about and click "Next".

If you do not have a wireless router around or you do not want to connect to a wireless network at this stage, you can click on the "Skip" button. You can also click on "Back" at any time if you feel you want to adjust a setting in the previous window.

However, if you clicked the "Next" button, then you should be greeted with a screen that checks for and installs updates for the Raspbian OS and other applications on the Raspberry Pi. This will allow the Raspbian OS to get an updated Raspbian since it is regularly updated to fix identified bugs, improve performance and include new features. To accept installing these updates, you will have to click the "Next" button on the screen, otherwise, you can select the "Skip" button.

At this stage, you will have to be patient as the process can take a bit of time. When the updating process gets done, a window will pop up saying "System is up to date," you can now click the "Reboot" button to complete the process and restart the Raspberry Pi.

Introducing the Raspbian OS

At the restart, the Raspbian desktop OS will load up showing that your Raspberry Pi 4 has been successfully set up to run a Raspbian Buster OS.

Figure 22: Raspbian Desktop

After the Raspbian starts up, you will be greeted with the Raspbian desktop with different icons, images, and menus.

Understanding the Desktop

The main screen of the Raspbian desktop is the one that has a picture showing the wallpaper in use.

The bar at the top is what is known as the taskbar. The icon at the top-far-left corner of the screen is the Raspberry Pi Icon or menu icon where you click to access the menu. When you click on it, you will find the installed applications in the various categories of the operating system. For each category like Programming, Education, Office, Internet, Sound & Video, Graphics, Games, and Accessories, you will see an arrow indicating that there are other specific programs in each of those categories, click on each of them to see what they have to offer. Also, besides the Raspberry

Icon are several other icons, which are as a group known as the launcher, which is understandable because it is from there you find quick access to launch various applications. On this menu icon, you will observe an icon representing the browser, another icon for File Manager, and other quick access to various programs.

Figure 23: Navigating the Menus

At the other end of the menu icons, to the right on the taskbar, are a set of other icons known as the system tray. The system tray includes various icons that include the

Bluetooth Icon, Network Icon, Volume Icon, CPU Monitor, Clock, and the Media Eject. Clicking the Media Eject button will allow you to safely eject and safely remove any removable storage device like the USB stick.

The clock icon, on the other hand, will bring up a calendar showing the present date and time. Next to the clock icon is the CPU Monitor Icon box with a line graph scrolling with a number in it, it is an indication of how hard the processor is working, with 0% indicating the system is doing nothing and 100% showing the CPU is being over labored.

The speaker icon is next, and it is utilized to adjust the Pi's audio volume. The network icon will reveal a list of nearby wireless networks, which is like the Bluetooth icon next to it for connecting to nearby Bluetooth devices.

Configuring the Raspberry Pi 4

To start using the Raspberry Pi 4, there are a few optional configurations that you have to be aware that you may have to do. These will enhance your use of the system and make you far more productive than if you did not perform them, some of them are pretty basic while a few of them are a little advanced and require devoting lots more attention to.

Therefore, let us dig right in and get started.

Connecting to the Internet

If want to use your Raspberry Pi to connect and access the internet, there are at least two options available on the device. That means you can choose to plug in an Ethernet cable into the Gigabit Ethernet port or to connect to the wireless network. The other option though not often used is to connect a USB modem to the USB port in areas that do not provide high-speed internet and are constrained to connect their modem with a SIM card as a means of accessing the internet.

When you connect the Ethernet cable to the Pi 4 as explained in chapter 3, Setting up the Hardware, you can instantly begin to browse as soon as the connection is established.

However, if you set up your wireless network during the installation of the operating system, you would most likely be already connected to that particular wireless network you used in setting it up. If, however, you skipped connecting to the wireless at that time or you are trying to connect to a different wireless router, then it is important to follow this process. To connect to a new wireless network, at least for the first time, you will need to click on the wireless network icon on the taskbar, at the top right-hand corner of the screen and select your network from the drop-down menu that appears. Once the wireless network is selected from the list, you will be prompted to enter the password or pre-shared key for the network assuming it is a secured network. You should only always connect to a secured network anyway. Once the connection has been established, the wireless network icon will change from the previous icon showing not connected to this new icon that indicates it is now broadcasting.

Setting up the Sound System

The Raspberry Pi 4 does not require a particular sound card to give out sounds. It can send the sound to a TV screen that has speakers built-in already, through its micro-HDMI to HDMI cable connection or an analog headphone jack. To set up the sound systems, right-click on the sound icon on the system tray and choose to either use the HDMI or analog options for hearing the sounds.

If all you desire to accomplish is adjust the volume of the sound, you can just click on the speaker icon (not right-click this time) and adjust the volume by moving the slider down to reduce the volume and up to increase the volume.

Setting up your Mouse and the Keyboard

You may be saying, hey wait a minute, I thought you said the Raspbian OS was just like its Windows and macOS counterpart, what is this option to start configuring the mouse and keyboard before it can work? Shouldn't it be a simple plug and play?

Yes mate, you are right, it is plug and play. You plug your mouse or keyboard whether it is the official one from Raspberry Pi or not and start working right away. However, if you want to configure a few things in those settings, then that is when you need to bother about this part of the Raspberry Pi configuration.

To configure your keyboard and mouse, you have to click the menu or Raspberry icon on the launcher (left corner of the taskbar, at the top of the screen), and select "Preferences" from the dropdown menu, and then "Mouse and Keyboard Settings" from the menu (Menu>Preferences>Mouse and Keyboard Setting). You will be greeted with two tabs where you can choose the Mouse or Keyboard tabs to configure any of them.

The default tab selected is the mouse tab, where you can adjust the motion or speed at which the mouse pointer moves on the screen by sliding the slider between the Fast and Slow slider. You can also adjust how fast you need to be double-clicking the mouse for the system to identify it as a double click. Please note that if it is too fast, you will have to double click really fast for it to work, in the same way, if it is too slow, you may find yourself double-clicking icons even when all you required was to click two independent events.

You can also swap the left and right mouse buttons to alter their functions, especially for left-handed people. You can click "Ok" to retain your changes and "Cancel" to neglect the changes. You may need to play around with it for a while to find out what works best for you.

To adjust your keyboard settings, you should click the Keyboard tab on the options at the top of the Mouse and Keyboard Settings.

Two things in the character repeat section that you can configure are the Repeat delay and the Repeat interval.

The repeat delay is what controls how the Raspberry Pi 4 responds when the keys are pressed and held on a computer keyboard, and how long before the Pi interprets it to mean that you want more than one instance of that character displayed on the screen. In other words, after the time set on the slider, the key will start repeating itself and spew out the characters across the screen. That pause between when the key is pressed and when it begins to start repeating those characters is the repeat delay.

The repeat rate, on the other hand, represents the speed with which those characters repeat themselves after the keys have been held down. You can set it here to be fast so that more characters are displayed at a shorter duration or slow so that the number of characters displayed becomes slower.

You can also decide to change the layout of your keyboard here to fit the layout of your keyboard for your country. As soon as you become satisfied with your settings, you can click the "Ok" button to confirm your changes or use the "Cancel" button to ignore whatever changes you may have made.

Using the Chromium Web Browser

If you have used Google Chrome or any other browser for that matter, you will be instantly familiar with the Chromium browser that comes with the Raspberry Pi 4. The browser allows you to access the internet easily. You are however not limited to this browser as you can decide to download other browsers like Firefox to browse with. You can see Chromium as the default browser that comes with the Raspbian OS, just like Microsoft edge that comes with Windows 10 and Safari that comes with the macOS.

Chromium can be used to browse the internet and visit various websites to play videos, access games, visit forums, send emails and access social media sites. You can easily maximize, minimize and expand the browser by clicking the various icons on the top-right corner of the taskbar.

The address bar is where you put the address of whatever site you intend to visit, this is like every other browser available and very straight forward.

If you want to have several pages open within the same browser, you can use the tab button at the top beside the last tab in the list or hold down the CTRL key on the keyboard before pressing the T key at the same time on your keyboard. The close button at the top right of the window is what is used to close the browser.

Exploring the File Manager

The Raspbian OS stores all the installed files on the MicroSD card. The File Manager is what enables users to access those files and directories and other files on other disks that may be externally connected to the Raspberry Pi 4 like the USB Flash Drive or Hard disk. You can select the File Manager from the group of icons in the launcher or click the menu icon and select "Accessories" from the list of categories that show up. When the File Manager is opened, it will take you to the Home (Pi) directory. This is where various file types are stored in a series of folders (directories) and subfolders (subdirectories).

The File Manager window is divided into two panes; the left pane that shows the folders on the Raspberry Pi and the right pane that shows the files and subfolders within that folder selected on the left pane.

The major subfolders in the Home directories are:

Desktop: This is the folder where the files and folder that come with Raspbian are loaded. Files stored here will show up on the Raspbian desktop.

Documents: The Documents folder is where most of the files you create are going to be stored

Downloads: This is the folder where downloaded files from the internet using the Chromium web browser will automatically be stored.

Music: This folder can be used to store songs for easy access.

Pictures: This folder is best suited for storing pictures or image files.

Public: Raspbian just like other Linux distributions generally treat most of your files as private, but files kept in the Public folder are going to be available to other users of the Raspberry Pi system when they login to their accounts.

Videos: Also suitable for storing videos and is the first place many video-playing programs will check when searching for a video to play.

Accessing Removable Drives on the Raspbian

Connecting drives to the USB port is a convenient way to backup and access files on the USB drives. When you insert a USB stick into your Raspberry Pi, a window will pop asking if you would like to have it opened in the File Manager, click "Ok" to confirm and the File Manager will show you all the files and directories inside it.

Word Processing and Productivity Suites for Raspberry Pi 4

One feature that many PCs have, irrespective of the operating system is to have a Word Processing application or tool. The most common application for this is Microsoft Word or the Office 365 productivity suite. If you consider the cost of getting a user license for this software in addition to the cost of the PC, then you will appreciate the fact that the Raspbian OS comes free with the LibreOffice which has the LibreOffice Writer as part of the software installed by default. The LibreOffice Writer is very similar to

Microsoft Word and Google Docs that you may presumably be used to.

A word processor like LibreOffice Writer, Microsoft Word, and Google Docs do not only allow you write a document but also to arrange, format, change the font, change color, insert images, add charts, insert table, add special effects and even allow for them to be printed.

To access the LibreOffice Writer, click the icon menu on the taskbar, move the mouse pointer to Office and click on LibreOffice Writer to open the word processor.

When selecting LibreOffice Writer, you will find that it is only one of the other productivity suites LibreOffice has to offer. The others when compared to their Microsoft Office Suites include:

LibreOffice Base: This is like Microsoft Access and is a valuable tool for storing information in a database.

LibreOffice Calc: This is a spreadsheet application and equally as powerful as Microsoft Excel in the handling and manipulation of numbers, creating charts and plotting graphs.

LibreOffice Draw: This is an illustrative program for creating pictures and diagrams.

LibreOffice Impress: This is like Microsoft PowerPoint and very useful for creating slide shows and running powerful presentations.

LibreOffice Math: This is a formula editor and an effective tool for creating advanced mathematical equations that can then be used by LibreOffice Writer or other applications.

Installing New Applications

Raspbian OS equally allows for the installation of other applications beyond the ones that come installed with it. You can download and install various other applications on the Raspberry Pi. While it is possible to install applications using text commands on the Raspbian terminals, which we will introduce in a subsequent series of this book, you can use GUI to install the Raspbian OS. To take advantage of this, your Raspberry Pi must be connected to the internet.

Figure 24: Accessing the Preferences Menu on the Raspbian

Now to start, you can click "Preferences" from the menu icon and then "Recommended software", you can then

78

browse through the different recommended software and filter each of them by their respective categories.

Once you have identified an application that you want to install or one that performs a function you want, you can click the checkbox on its right side and click "Ok" to install.

While Raspberry's Pi recommended software is a great resource for sourcing software to install, there are a lot of other libraries of other available programs and applications that users can use to install their preferred applications.

To access those packages, access the "Preferences" again from the menu icon and select the Add/ Remove Software in the menu, search for the particular software or browse to check for a suitable one across the different categories from the left menu and take "Ok" to begin the installation process.

To uninstall or remove an existing program or software, you also access the Add/Remove Software the same way of adding and remove the checkmark on the one we want to remove and then take "ok" and the program will be uninstalled.

Let us try to experiment with this by installing a very useful, open-source and powerful graphical application called GIMP.

Consequently, you access the Add/ Remove Software from the Menu Icon> Preferences> Add/ Remove Software

Type 'GIMP' into the search box and press Enter.

Select the checkbox to the right of the application that appears on the list and click "OK" to begin the installation process.

To be sure you are the admin and owner authorizing the installation, you will be prompted for your password, enter your password on the screen provide if you have previously changed your password, but if you are yet to change your password, you can use the default password 'raspberry'.

The installation process will presumably require you to confirm you want to go on with it by typing, "Y" for yes and the process will continue. You will see a series of codes go up the screen, not to worry, they have nothing to do with you, just wait for it to do its thing and after which the installation process will be complete.

Configure Raspberry Pi

The preference section is where you can handle other aspects of your Raspberry Pi 4 settings. It is here you are able to control many of your Raspberry Pi's settings, like the password. You can access these settings on Menu Icon> Preferences > Raspberry Pi Configuration.

The configuration tool is split into four tabs, where each of them handles an aspect of the Raspbian OS. The first of these when you start up the configuration tool is System, which is where you change the Pi's password and perform other operations.

Next after the Systems tab is the Interface Tab. The settings on this tab are all set to be disabled by default and only need to be changed when you are adding new hardware like the Raspberry Pi Camera Module and which should be done only if the manufacturer request it. The SSH is, however, exempted from this rule. Other tabs include the performance and the localization tab.

System

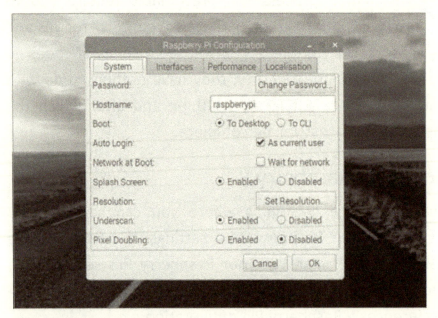

Figure 25: Configuration Tool on the Raspbian

This tab allows you to tweak some basic settings in your Pi 4 operating system. Some of the settings you can configure on the System's tab include:

Password: You can set or change the password of your account with this function.

81

Boot: This is where you decide if you want either of the Desktop or CLI (command line interface) to be the one that shows up when your Raspberry Pi 4 starts-up. Many beginners will naturally prefer the Desktop to be the default.

Auto Login: If you enable this option, your Raspberry Pi will not require a password during startup, instead it will log in automatically whenever it starts. This will be useful for systems usually unmanned and in remote locations.

Network at Boot: You should only select this option if you want your Raspberry Pi 4 to start only if there is a network connection available. This will be valuable for situations where the Raspberry Pi 4 needs to work in a network environment by sending and receiving data as part of its operation.

Splash Screen: You can use this to set if your startup message (also called splash) is to show up when your Raspberry Pi is booted.

Interfaces

This is where you configure your Raspberry Pi 4's connection to other devices and components. On this interface tab, you can decide which interfaces to turn on and which ones to turn off.

You can link devices and components to the Raspberry Pi utilizing various types of connections. The Interfaces tab is where you turn these various connections on or off so that the Pi can recognize when a connection is linked. By default, they are turned off. The components you can configure here include:

Camera: This is utilized to enable the Raspberry Pi Camera Module.

SSH: This is employed to enable access to your Raspberry Pi remotely using SSH from another computer.

VNC: This is used to enable access to your Raspberry Pi Desktop using VNC from another computer

SPI: You implement this function to enable SPI GPIO pins on the board

I2C: You use this function to enable the I2C GPIO pins on the board

Serial: You use this function to enable the Serial (RX, TX) GPIO pins

1-Wire: This is utilized to enable the 1-Wire GPIO pin

Remote GPIO: This is used to allow access to your Raspberry Pi's 4 GPIO pins from another computer

Performance

This is one part of the Raspbian setting you have to be careful about when playing around with the settings because this configuration can make your system behavior erratic if not properly handled.

But if you were to ever want to change some CPU parameters for a project, this would be the place to do it, by changing the performance settings of your Pi 4.

Overclock: You can use this feature to change the speed and voltage of the CPU to improve performance.

GPU Memory: This function is used to alter the amount of memory given to the GPU.

Localization

This is the section where you can modify your Raspberry Pi settings to reflect the region you are localized.

Locale: This setting is used to set the language, character set, and country where the Raspberry Pi is being used.

Time zone: You can select your time zone here.

Keyboard: You can select your keyboard layout here.

Wi-Fi Country: Here, you can also select the Wi-Fi's country code

Updating your Pi

Updating your Raspbian OS frequently is a smart way to ensure your OS has the latest features and fixes meant to address security loopholes. It is always best practice to first refresh the software package list before installing any update.

The update function can be found in the menu icon> preferences > Add/ Remove Software > Options > Refresh Package Lists

When that is performed, you can check for and install updates for the, menu icon> preferences > Add/ Remove Software > Options > Check for Updates.

The Package Updater will then check if there are updates available and displays whatever it finds. You can then click "Install Updates" to install all the available updates.

As expected, the Raspbian will prompt you to enter your password, if you have previously changed your password, now is a good time to put your new password, otherwise, it will be 'raspberry'.

After that, the software will then download the required updates which will then be installed. This process can take anything between 10 mins to 30mins, however, you can monitor the status of the installation by looking at the progress bar at the bottom left-hand corner.

Introducing the Raspbian Terminal

Anyone that wants to learn about Raspberry Pi in-depth will ultimately have to learn how to operate the terminal in performing some required level of scripting, but because this book is only interested in getting you started, only a basic introduction will be done in this case.

You can use the terminal to do useful kinds of stuff; you can use it to navigate file directories, control the Raspberry Pi 4 and perform advanced kinds of functions that instead of clicking the functions in some fanciful Graphical User Interface (GUI), you will be typing commands to get things accomplished.

To open a terminal window, you click on the Terminal icon on the launcher or click the menu icon> Accessories > Terminal.

To use the terminal, you simply type the proper command into the terminal window and tell it to run by pressing the "Enter" key, just like in the old days when computers were just starting.

Let's try out a few commands now.

In the terminal window, type: "ls", followed by the "Enter" key.

You will see a list of all the files and subdirectory in the current file directory which by default is the Home (pi) directory.

To change directory, all you need to do is type the command "cd" followed by the name of the directory we want to change to. This will be all we would do for now, if you love to be notified when the next book that explains how to use Raspbian Linux comes out, you can go to the website   https://lindashift.wixsite.com/linuxtutorial   and subscribe to be alerted when you get your copy.

Shutting Down the Raspberry Pi 4

Now that you have gone through the various sections of the Raspbian Desktop, you must now learn how to shut it down, which is a very important feature of the Raspbian OS, in ensuring it is safely shut down.

The shutdown process is useful for ensuring all your important documents get saved on the non-volatile memory like the MicroSD so that you do not lose your data on the volatile memory when Raspberry Pi is shut down.

To shut down your Raspberry Pi 4, click on the raspberry icon on the taskbar, do not forget the raspberry icon is also called the menu, select Shutdown from the dropdown and a window with three options will show up, select the Shutdown option from them. The OS will initiate the shutting down process and ensure that all relevant system files go to where they are supposed to be. You will have to wait for a few seconds after the display has gone black, for the flashing green light on the Pi to also go off before switching off the power supply.

However, although it is fashionable to perform the shutdown function, the Raspberry Pi is rugged enough to be switched off directly from the power source without causing any significant damage to the OS, unlike other operating systems that may begin to experience some problems if a proper shutdown is not done. Do not forget that the Raspberry Pi 4 can be installed and used in certain applications that may not have any form of display, so just switching it off may be your best way of shutting it down. Raspbian OS has been designed to handle that.

Apart from the shutdown option, you can also select the reboot option which will basically go through the shutdown process and instead of shutting the system down will restart the Raspberry Pi 4.

The logout option is only useful if the Pi 4 is set up to have more than one user, so logging off one user will allow another user to log in.

Chapter 7

Introduction to Programming

While it is important to note that the Raspberry Pi 4 can be used as a Desktop computer, but that is not all that the system is designed for, as a matter of fact, It was designed to be used to teach students how to learn to program in a not too daunting way. Raspberry Pi 4's Raspbian comes pre-installed with Python and Scratch programming environments.

When you start programming Raspberry Pi 4 with Scratch, you do not need to have any previous programming experience because Scratch will make programming the Raspberry Pi 4 a seamless, easy and interesting experience.

Introducing the Scratch Program

Scratch is a good introductory way to get into programming because it is a visual programming language that allows you to design and create games, animations, interactive stories, and other interesting applications. Raspberry Pi extends the use of Scratch in the creation of highly innovative products and projects.

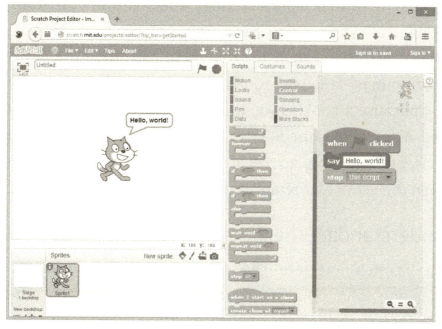

Figure 26: Scratch Programming Software Interface

It was first developed in 2003 at MIT to be a programming language where you use blocks of codes in creating programs from a set of pre-written blocks enclosed in color-coded jigsaw pieces. Although Scratch is designed to have a very friendly appearance and easy to be understood by a typical 3rd or 4th grader, it is still a functional and powerful programming environment for people of all ages to use it as a way of learning the basics of programming simply and enjoyably. Scratch can be used in the creation of simple games, animations and complex interactive robotic projects using Raspberry Pi 4.

Unlike many other programming environments like Java, Python, and C++, Scratch involves dragging, dropping and combining various blocks of codes when writing a program. Using predefined codes means you are not going to have syntax errors in your programming. Scratch is a good programming language to start using with your Raspberry Pi 4 because it enables you to get started in as little as a day and helps you learn how to think creatively, understand concepts and how to collaborate effectively. When you open the Scratch program, it opens to a project window.

Understanding the Scratch Interface

The Scratch interface can sometimes be confusing for someone who does not understand the interface. The interface is divided into panes or areas, with each pane having a specific function.

Objects in Scratch are called sprite and are the characters on the screen that you try to control with a Scratch program. The default sprite is a cat. You can easily select other sprites. Sprites have to be programmed to act in Scratch. Such actions can be moving, jumping, speaking, etc.

The backdrop on the window where a sprite can be manipulated is known as the Stage. It is in this area that the sprites move around the stage in response to the commands in your program.

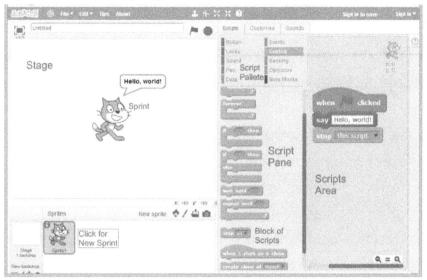

Figure 27: Description of Scratch Interface

The Scripts pane is the section that houses the blocks of code or scripts that are used in projects.

Scripts are the codes that can be dragged and placed on the Scratch workspace window. You can either set a trigger event that will get the scripts running or have it triggered by double-clicking the first block of script.

The Scripts Area is where you combine the blocks of scripts by dragging and dropping blocks from the block scripts pane.

At any instance, new sprites and backdrops can be removed or added to a project and made to be associated with their respective script sequences or programs.

Scripts

Scripts are the action codes that are used for making the sprites do what we want them to do. To make the long list of scripts easy to access and use, they have been categorized and grouped into different categories using different colors for each category to represent scripts that perform similar actions. The act of grouping makes the scripting process a lot more manageable. So, if you want to make your sprite perform an action then you simply identify which of the ten categories best represents what you are trying to achieve, and chances are you will find the one that suits what you want there.

Categories of Scripts

Motion

The scripts in the motion structure block are used to move, position, rotate and control the movement of a sprite, including how to react when it reaches the edge of the screen.

Control

The control block structures contain scripts that impose conditional statements on the program that include if-then blocks, if-then-else blocks, repeat loops, wait, if-then and if-then-else. These blocks of code make a program more intelligent and able to make decisions. These scripts help a program determine what next steps to take based on a prevailing condition. It is also the first script to initiate the start of a program.

Looks

These scripts in this category are used to change the way a sprite looks including having their costume changed and hidden during the animation.

Sound

These scripts are used to play various applicable sounds. They are also used to stop, change the volume and tempo of the assigned sound.

Events

The scrips here are used to tell a block of code to execute when an event happens. Examples of such events can include clicking the start flag, pressing a specific keyboard key, clicking a sprite, pressing a mouse or responding to a broadcast that will, in turn, activate your sprites and cause them to react.

Pen

The scripts are used to allow the user to write or draw. By moving the pen up or down, various shakes can be drawn on the screen.

Sensing

These sets of scripts enable programs to be able to sense when things interact with the system and with each other. They can be used when the mouse is used to control each of sprite or when the sprite touches each other. They are also used for interactions and getting input from the environment. This is extremely useful for robotics, games, and animations.

Operators

These scripts are used to compare values, perform arithmetic expressions, generate random numbers and record the number of times an activity has been conducted to trigger an operation based on the outcome of the operation. It can be used by simple games in creating random outputs to make random choices every time the game is played.

Data

You find this script very useful for setting variables that are then used to keep score and track how long a game has been in play.

More Blocks: this is the part that allows you to include custom blocks of your choice. This is a very important block as you will get to discover later on that it can be used to generate the extension for the blocks that are useful for configuring the GPIO of the Raspberry Pi.

Scripts are an important aspect of Scratch and are what give it a tremendous amount of power and flexibility in creating advanced projects. By combining the different blocks, various outcomes can be achieved.

Sprite Programming with Control, Motion, Looks, and Sounds

Control blocks

You can always identify a Control block with the orange or yellow color from the categories of blocks from the script panes. The control block has the option of making use of either of three blocks for programming. The available options include:

1) When the green flag is clicked - This control block is used to start a project when you click the green flag in the upper right corner.

2) When space key is pressed - This control block is used to start a project when the space bar is pressed. You can decide not to use the space bar by clicking the black dropdown and choose a different key.

3) When sprite 1 is clicked - T This control block is used to start a project when the sprite on stage is clicked.

To start, you will have to drag and drop the control block into the scripts area. It is to this control block that you will connect the next block like the next piece of the puzzle.

Motion blocks

These blocks have a blue label and belong to the blue category of scripts. They are used to move sprites in various positive and negative directions and can be used to also move them at various angles and degrees.

1) Move 10 steps: This motion will move the sprite 10 steps in the positive direction. That value can however be changed to any value you want. You can also move the sprite backward by using negative values instead of positive values.

Glide__sec to x:___ y:____ : This motion block can be used to move a sprite and glide to a specified position using coordinates in X number of seconds. This is useful for animation and you can control how fast it will take for the sprite to get to the desired destination by controlling the time. To know the XY coordinates of a position by moving the sprite to the desired position during the programming and then copying the values you find at the top of the script area.

Looks blocks

These are the blocks that fall into the purple category labels of the scripts in the script area and it has several blocks that are used to control what the sprite says or look.

1) Say "hello" for 2 seconds: This will allow you to program the sprite to display a word bubble that will display what you have typed. This content is also changeable by filling the white space and create a conversation that those familiar with comics should be used to.

2) Switch to costume - Many sprites have more than many costumes which you can see if you clicked the "Costumes" tab beside the Scripts. Sprites can be programmed to switch their costume and in situations where the sprite have only one costume in its library, scratch allows you to create a custom one-clicking copy and then edit to paint and create a new costume.

Sound blocks

These are the blocks that fall into the fuchsia label and belong to the fuchsia category of scripts. They are used to program spites to produce sounds or words that are audible. The sound tab is close to costumes and you can also import or record new sounds. You can use it for special effects or animal sounds and any other sound you can imagine.

Choosing a new sprite

The cat is not the only type of sprite available to use in scratch even though it is the default one. You can delete the cat or any other sprite at any time clicking the scissors icon at the top of the stage and then selecting the sprite.

Another way to do it is to right-click the thumbnail and then click delete.

When you want to select a new sprite, you need to use one of the three available options: You have to: import, paint a new sprite or use a random sprite.

New sprite: You can double click on any category of sprites to choose the one you to wish to use.

Paint a new sprite: This allows you to create a sprite yourself using a paintbrush, lines, circles, basic shapes and paint bucket in creating your own custom sprite.

Create random sprite: With this function, Scratch will randomly select a sprite for you.

Selecting a Background

The stage thumbnail is where you select a new background for your project. You do that when you click on the background, from where you can paint or import any background of your choice. You can also use your computer webcam to take a picture of yourself and use it as a background or you can paint and create a drawing with the paint editor.

You can also import available backgrounds by double-clicking any of the folders and choosing a background of your choice.

Examples of Scratch Projects

Project 1: Hello World

If you do not already have Scratch opened, you can load Scratch on Pi just like any other program by going through the raspberry icon to open up the menu and then the programming section and click on Scratch 2. A few seconds later and the user interface will be loaded on the screen.

With scratch, you do not need to write lines of codes, instead, you click the various blocks and drag them to the screen when writing programs.

Most people down the ages have always used "Hello World" as their introduction into the programming world, so we will try and keep the tradition that many programming experts in the world have gone through before us.

Start by clicking the "Looks" category from among the different categories in the block's palette, which will bring up the different blocks within that category. You will notice that they are all colored purple, that is because each category is colored differently so that it is easy to know what section they belong to.

Find the block that has, "Say Hello!" on it, click and then drag it to the script area of the screen before letting go with your mouse button. If you look closely, you will notice that the block has what looks like a hole at the top and a part that matches that type of hole sticking out at the bottom, as you would find in a jigsaw puzzle.

Figure 28: Say Hello Block

The hole at the top is an indication that the block requires another block at the top to fill it up, while the protruding section under indicates that it is also able to accept another block under it. For this program to work, we have to find a way to tell the Raspberry Pi 4 how to know that it should execute the "Say Hello" program, that thing is what is referred to as a trigger because it is what is used to initiate or activate the program to start.

Now for this program, let us create a trigger that we can use to activate it, for that we will need another block, but this time from the "Events" Category, the "Events" category can be found in the same palette you found the "Looks" category. The "Events" category is colored with a light shade of brown. Look for the block that is labeled "When Clicked" and has a green flag between the two words,

click it, and drag it to the script area above the "Say Hello" block. Fit the part of the block that sticks out from under and position it to fit into the hole on the "Say Hello" block.

Figure 29: Hello Block with Trigger Block

You will notice that this block does not have a hole at the top like the "Say Hello" had and instead, it has a shape at the top that looks like a man wearing a hat which is why it is sometimes referred to as a hat block.

To test the program, we have to run the program. To run this program, we have to click the green flag icon at the top of the stage area, which should start the program since the trigger was set to "when 'Green Flag' clicked", if everything is okay, then the sprite (Cat) will greet you with a "Hello!".

You see how easy it was, that is why Scratch is the favorite program for many beginners and a good way to introduce kids to programming because they love colored objects and it is quite easy for them to follow.

You can now save your project by clicking Save from the file menu.

You have now successfully created your first Scratch Project Program.

Project 2: Move Sprite Forward

The Hello project was just to get us started with Scratch, rarely in real life do projects have just one action, many projects are usually a sequence of activities lined up, one after the other. That is why most computer programs are defined as a list of instructions, starting from top to bottom that follow each other in a logical order or linear sequence.

We will start by creating a new project from the File menu. We should have a new slate to perform our operation, next drag the "When Clicked" with a green flag in between to the script area to start our program. Now click on the "Motion" category in the blocks palette to expose all the scripts in the blue category. Next click, drag and move the "move 10 steps" block to the script area. This script tells your sprite to move 10 steps in the positive direction as soon as it is triggered.

Now, let us run the program to test what we have done. Click the green flag icon at the top of the stage area icon, which should start the program to test the program, if everything goes well, the sprite should move 10 steps in the forward direction when you run the program after which it will stop.

Figure 30: Learning to Move Sprite 10 Steps Forward

Now, let us try to make the sprite work continuously until we manually stop it, which is where the control block comes into play. The control block is the yellow category of scripts. To make the sprite move indefinitely, you will need to use the "Forever" script, click it and drag it into the script area to start using it and put it under the "When Click" block with the green flag in-between. You can run the system now to test it, remember, testing it involves clicking the green flag at the top of the stage area. You will notice that unlike the previous system where the sprite stopped moving after it had moved 10 steps, this program will keep moving the sprite indefinitely until you click the red flag beside the green flag, or it gets to the end of the screen. So, let us stop it now and see how we can add more blocks of scripts to the program so that the program can be made to perform more advanced functions.

104

Let us try to control how the sprite reacts when it gets to the end of the screen by adding another block to it. Still on the motion category, click and drag "if on edge, bounce" to the script area, directly under the "move 10 steps" block. It should look like the image in figure 32.

Figure 32: Learning to Deal with Screen Edges

You can now run it to see how it bounces back when played. How did it perform?

You may have noticed the sprite turns upside down when moving to the other end of the screen but goes upright when going in the positive direction. To make it move with the correct orientation in both directions, here is what you should do. When the sprite turns upside down, press the red button beside the green flag to stop the movement, click the image of the sprite about the script area and try to rotate the sprite.

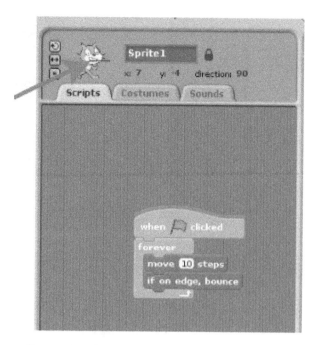

Figure 33: Change the Direction of the Sprite

Play around in this area until the sprite faces the correct direction. Notice the blue line extending from the sprite, it is what you will use for the rotation and manipulation of the sprite. As you soon as you are able to get the sprite to face the right direction, you can now test run it.

Okay, let us now make it move around all the edges of the screen by adding another block from the motion category, remember? The blue ones.

Look out for the block with the label "turn 30 degrees", when you find it, click and drag it above the "forever" block in the script area. You can also now run it to see how it operates. Stop it now when you are satisfied with its performance. Let us take it a notch further.

Let us make the sprite draw a line on any path it takes by adding another block from the pen category to the program. The pen category is the one with the green block. Pick and drag the "Pen Down" to the script area for it to trace the path the sprite moves by placing it above the forever block and below the "turn 30 degrees" block.

It should look like the image in figure 34.

Figure 34: Trace Lines with Pen Down

If you want to change the program such that the colors of the line changes on each iteration, we can tweak the code a bit to achieve that. The colors in the pen block are arranged in a sequence which is what makes it possible for the colors to change along the way. The colors are arranged in 200 shades of color, ranging from 0 to 199, colors above 200 will wrap around.

To do that you will add another block of script that tells it to change colors by 1. Let's add it to the script area now. If you are satisfied with your work, you can save it now.

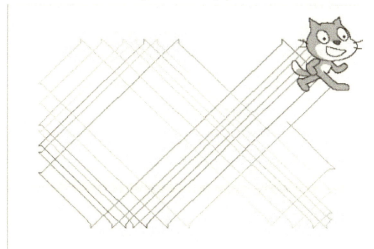

Figure 36: Outcome of Changing Lines Color

Project 3: The power of variables and conditionals

Sometimes when writing a program, you want the program to be able to store data that you can retrieve later in the program or to modify it in the course of the program. There are several inbuilt variables inside scratch programs that store data like the X-Y coordinates, pen color, color shade, and other inbuilt variables, however, users can also define their own variable to store user-defined data inside.

The values in a variable can change over time compared to constants that hold fixed values. A variable tends to have two major properties; its name and the value that it stores. The value stored can either be a number, text (strings), Boolean (true or false) or null (when it has no value). Variables are a very simple and powerful tool in any computer language. In short, it would have been practically impossible to write certain programs if the concept of variables was not available.

Variables are used in games to track their progress and determine the status of a character in the game and to know what stage and time the game is on.

Now let us start with a new project by clicking on New Project from the file menu.

Click the "When Click" with the green flag in between from the "Events" category and drag it to the screen.

Click on the "Data" category in the blocks palette and then click the "Make a Variable" button from the drop-down. For the variable name, we can use "test-loop" as the variable name, leave the option for "set for all sprites" and click ok to allow a series of blocks appear in the block's palette.

Note, you can name your variable whatever you like. As soon as the variable is named, you will see a set of blocks show up with various names under the data category, all of which include "test-loop" because that was what we named our variable, you can create more variables with different names to see the blocks that appear.

Figure 37: Learning to Set Variable Name

Click and drag the "set test-loop to 0" block to the script area under the "When Click" block for the program to initialize the variable with a value of 0.

Let us undertake the program further by adding a "repeat 10" block from the control category to it. Place it directly under the set "say test-loop for 2 secs" and change the value from 10 to 8. The repeat block is used to get the program to repeat a continuous set of actions, unlike the other linear ones that execute only once.

After that, you can click the "Say Hello! For 2 Secs" from the Looks category and drag it to the script area. Place it inside the repeat block.

This block by default will display Hello for 2 seconds and disappear, but you can alter what you want it to display by changing the text in the Hello part and for how long it should be displayed by changing the number of seconds. What happens to a situation when you want to use the same text across various other blocks? It would be clumsy to type it multiple times into all the blocks especially when you plan to change the text in the future. By using a variable, you can input the value once and use that variable many times.

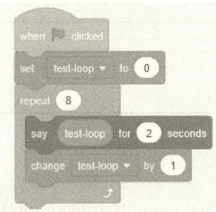

Figure 38: Using Variables Instead of Hard Coding

To achieve that, click and grab the rounded "test-loop" block which is known as reporter block at the top of the list on "Data" category in the blocks palette with the checkbox next to it over the word "Hello" in the block, which will

combine the two blocks together to form one new block "say test-loop for 2 secs".

Since the test-loop is initialized to 0, when the program is run by clicking the green flag on the stage area, the sprite will display a bubble showing '0' on the screen.

Add the "change test-loop by 1" block from the data category and position it under the "say test-loop for 2 secs" block. The script will keep changing the variable "test-loop" as the program runs by increasing the value by one on each iteration.

Run the program now to test it. The sprite will display different values on the display until it gets to 7 in spite of the fact that the repeat value was set to repeat 8 times, well that is because the first value that the test-loop variable was initialized to be 0, so by running from 0 -7, it would have iterated 8 times.

Let us increase the function of the program by adding another block to it, let us start by adding the "if-then" block from the control category in the block's palette. Click and drag it to the script area of your screen and position it under the "change test-loop by 1". After that, click the operator category and select the block that has two boxes with an equal to sign (=) between them. Drag that block and place it inside the diamond block on the top right part of the "if-then" block so that it looks like this figure 39. Notice that the shape of the block has a diamond shape, the same shape as the diamond shape in the "if-then" block.

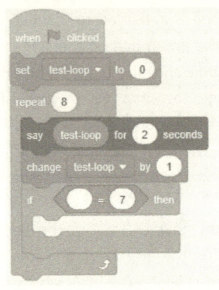

Figure 39: Combining the "If-then" Block with the Operator

The "if-then" block is one of the conditional blocks available on Scratch. Conditional blocks are scripts that only run when certain defined conditions have been met. Click the data category again and click and drag our variable we named "test-loop" earlier in our project into the first box in the "if-then" we put as in the image in figure 39. Now type "7" in the second box.

Next, let us click and drag the "say Hello! For 2 seconds" block inside the "if-then" block. Now, let us modify the content of the "say Hello! For 2 seconds" block by typing "We have reached the end" to replace the "Hello".

It is time to test the program by running it. The sprite should behave as before until the value gets to 7 after

113

which the conditional block will state, "We have reached the end".

If you achieved this successfully, you have just advanced your career in the programming world. You can save your work now.

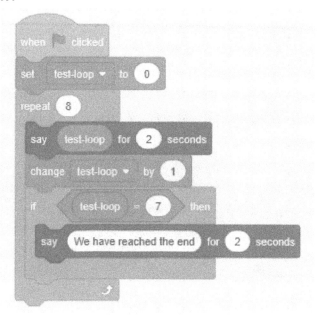

Figure 40: Complete Program for Project 3

Projects you can try

1. Create a new scratch program that outputs "I love this book" when it is run.
2. Create a new project that counts numbers from 1-20, when the numbers get to 15 up to 20, it should output "This value is too high for this program".

Chapter 8

Introducing Physical Computing Programming

The impression many people have when they think of programming or coding is to imagine that it to be only about programming or configuring software, however with Raspberry Pi, it is more than just programming or configuring a software like scratch or Phyton for the sake of it, instead it can be used to affect the real world through hardware. To get the most power out of the programming of Raspberry Pi 4, you want to be able to utilize it to develop various kinds of physical devices from simple LED controls, to robots, to motion detection, retro gaming consoles and many other sophisticated applications that affect various real-life problems. When you press a button on your TV or monitor the climatic conditions in your environment or activate the traffic light, you are involved in what is known as physical computing which is one area where the Raspberry Pi excels.

But for that to happen, the Pi 4 has to be able to communicate with the outside world, and the 40 GPIO pins of Raspberry Pi 4 are what makes that happen. The Raspberry Pi is a remarkable device for anyone who wants to learn physical computing which is why learning about the GPIO, its configuration and how it works is incredibly important.

Configuring the GPIO as Input and Output Pins

The Raspberry Pi 4 comes with 40 male GPIO pins and each of these pins allow different configuration, functions, and uses. They take one section on the Raspberry Pi 4 board and can easily be located on the Pi 4 board where they sit on two long rows of metal pins on the board. It is with these pins that you can connect various types of hardware which can then be controlled via the software, which in this case will be with Scratch. By programming Scratch, you can manipulate the devices connected to the Pi 4 and make them do as you wish. For example, you can create a circuit that has a switch to put on an LED, switch it off after a few minutes and any other thing you desire it to do.

Some other learning boards have certain pins as outputs and other pins as inputs, but not so with the Raspberry Pi in general, and with Raspberry Pi 4 particularly, there is no fixed purpose to which way the pins can be put to use. Having pins on a board exposed in the manner they are on a Raspberry Pi 4 is what is referred to as headers.

However, not all the pins are directly available for use in your projects because some are them are used to provide power, others are reserved for more specific functions like communicating with other physical add-on hardware.

GPIO pins on the Raspberry board can only be in one of two states, high or low, on or off and this can be set at the software level using the programming application. The most common programming languages used in controlling the state and direction of pins are with programming languages like Python, JavaScript, Scratch and a host of others. The pins can be programmed to be in a state of either being receptive to current or giving out current.

Irrespective of what you intend to develop, knowing the architecture of the GPIO pins is a vital knowledge to have as a programmer in understanding the Raspberry Pi GPIO pin layout and a description of what each pin is used for.

Some pins on the board are the power pins, others provide grounds for the circuit, while some are for I2C, UART, SPI and some connect to other interfaces. Suffice to say that the GPIO on the Raspberry Pi 4 board carries out various functions.

The operating voltage that the GPIO uses is 3.3V with an allowable maximum current of 16mA, which means that anything that requires a larger current will need to use an external add-on or component that to manage the process so that the board does not get damaged.

GPIO Pin Layout

To appreciate how the pins on the GPIO are arranged, you have to first position it such that the closest pin to where the MicroSD is identified and used as pin 1 to reference the others. This pin provides 3.3V power. To the right of that pin is pin2 with an output power of 5V. Therefore, in that manner, the pins are numbered downward with the pins on the left being the odd-numbered ones while the ones on the right being the even-numbered ones. That means the pins on the left will have an odd number sequence of 1,3,5,6.... 39, while the ones on the right will have an even number sequence of 2,4,5..., 40.

This type of numbering is known as the physical addressing and is the simplest way of referencing the pins on a board, however, at the software level, the pins have their own addresses.

The official way of identifying pins on the GPIO board is using a system called Broadcom (BCM) pin numbering nomenclature. The pins on this numbering system use the prefix BCM or GPIO before the number as part of the addressing system. Although it can be confusing to have pins on the physical board as pin 11 yet they are labeled as GPIO17 or BCM17, or pin 13 as GPIO22 or BCM22 and pin

15 as GPIO27 or BCM27, it is, however, the conventionally accepted way of numbering the respective pins on the GPIO. This system does not use the GPIO prefixes for the power pins like the 3.3V, 5V, and the Ground (GND) pins.

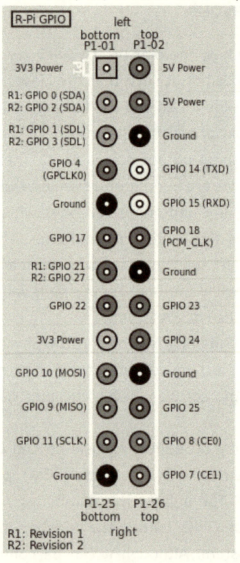

Figure 41: GPIO Pin Layout on a Raspberry Pi 4 Board

Certain GPIO pins also have alternate functions that allow them to interface with various kinds of devices that use the I2C, SPI or UART protocols. For example, GPIO2 and GPIO3 can be used to connect devices using the I2C protocol, while GPIO9 and GPIO10 can be used to connect devices using the SPI protocol.

However, to be able to use these pins with these protocols for these functions, they will have to be enabled on their interfaces on the configuration feature of the Raspbian OS on which the Raspberry Pi is running. You can enter the configuration tool on the Raspbian OS from the menu icon.

I2C - Inter-Integrated Circuit

Certain devices use the low speed two-wire serial protocol of the I2C standard. I2C uses SDA and SCL as its two connections with the SDA pin being the component that transmits data to and from the connection while the SLI pin is the component that controls the speed. Devices that employ this standard use a master-slave relationship and as a quick and easy way to connect various devices like LCD or LED screens, A/D converters, and temperature sensors.

The I2C protocol is a vital skill to acquire because of how useful it is in learning how to connect high precision sensors.

UART - Universal Asynchronous Receiver / Transmitter

This protocol provides an alternative way of connecting or communicating with the Raspberry Pi 4 without a keyboard or pointing device in what is known as a headless setup. The UART pins, in this case, provide a console or terminal login by using a serial cable or USB cable from a PC as an alternative for connecting when a network connection is not used. It has to be enabled in the Raspberry Pi configuration from the settings menu also to be able to provide a reliable means of communication without the need to purchase any other equipment. It is however very rarely utilized.

SPI - Serial Peripheral Interface

The SPI is another similar protocol to the I2C because of the presence of a master-slave relationship between the Raspberry Pi and devices that connect to it.

Determining Whether to use I2C, SPI or UART

The information on the datasheet of a device will instruct you which of the specific connection type to use. So, a device like an LED screen may require SPI protocol whereas another LED screen might need the I2C protocol, which is why reading the documentation on a product is what is used to determine what Pi pin to use.

The Raspberry Pi 4 has more I2C, SPI and UART pins available than previous Raspberry Pi, which can be activated using device tree overlays to get four additional SPI, I2C, and UART connections.

Ground (GND)

In electronics, this is used to refer to the reference point of 0V from which all other voltages are measured. It is utilized to complete an electrical circuit when devices are connected to a power source. For example, if an LED is connected to the 5V on the GPIO, essentially through a resistor, the other end has to be connected to ground (Gnd, gnd, common, 0V) for the circuit to be complete.

It is always best practice to connect your device to ground first before connecting it to power especially when the device involved is a sensitive piece of equipment.

Ground is also frequently referred to as GND, common, gnd or negative, but they all mean the same thing.

They are eight ground connections points on the GPIO and all of them are common which means that any of them can be used at any time interchangeably depending on which of them is convenient.

5V

The 5v pin on the GPIO provides access to 5v supply directly from the mains adaptor while providing power for the Raspberry Pi 4 itself. Devices that require 5V can be powered from these pins directly and appropriate care has to be taken to ensure that the input voltage and connection is correct because any bypass with a voltage that is higher than the specified one could destroy the raspberry pi 4 since the pins do not enjoy the fuse and voltage regulation safety feature provided by the Pi 4.

There are two 5V pins on a Raspberry Pi 4 board and both are permanently on (high).

3.3V

The internal voltage of the Raspberry Pi 4 is 3.3V which is also the voltage that pins with this output are labeled with. Just like the 5V, there are two of the 3.3V pins on the board, although they tend to be rarely used, only often used when testing certain devices to ascertain that they are good when building circuits.

GPIO XX

These are the available pins for programming and are identified with numbers from 2 to 27. Therefore, you can have labels of pins as GPIO2, GPIO3 …. GPIO27

ID EEPROM

GPIO pins that have the labels ID EEPROM are pins that are reserved for use with Hardware Attached on Top (HAT) and some other accessories that adapt to it.

Electrical Components

To use the Raspberry Pi 4 to develop electronic devices, it has to be combined with various electrical components like sensors (proximity, temperature, motion, etc.), LEDs, ICs and many other discrete and integrated components. All these devices can then be controlled through the GPIO header from the programming software.

Breadboard

One profoundly integral component that many hobbyists have in their armory of equipment is the breadboard, also known by the name solderless breadboard. Down the ages, long before the advent of Raspberry Pi 4, breadboard has been in existence and has been used as a way of testing out circuit designs to ensure they are working without having to solder the components on the board.

The breadboard comes with standard holes that have sections linked to make it easy to connect electrical components. Therefore, instead of having to connect many devices with wires, a breadboard is used instead by inserting the various components into positions on the board from where they can connect with other devices using the metal track linking the different holes.

The breadboard equally has a track section dedicated to power distribution all of which makes it a lot easier to develop circuits. You can definitely build, modify and move from one design to another with the use of a breadboard and try out different variations of a circuit to come up with the best solution for what you are trying to do. This is one of the reasons why it is a valuable electrical component to have when building circuits.

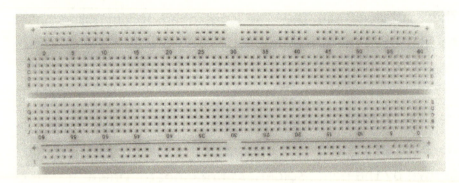

Figure 42: Breadboard

Jumper Wires

Jumpers represent another effective component to have when working with the physical computing side of working with Raspberry Pi 4. These cables enable you to connect various components to the Raspberry Pi 4 whether or not you are using the breadboard. Jumper cables are available in three types that include male-to-female (M2F), Female-2-Femail (F2F) and the Male-to-Male (M2M).

The male-to-female (M2F) cables are used to connect pins on the Raspberry Pi to a breadboard, while the female-2-female (F2F) cables are very useful in connecting discrete components together often as an alternative to a breadboard. The male-2-male (M2M) is used to establish connections from one part of a breadboard to the other. They are equally an immensely functional component to have in your toolbox.

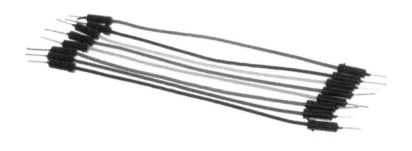

Figure 43: Jumper Cables

Push Button Switch

This is a momentary type of switch that can be used to put a device on and off. It can equally be utilized for fast switching applications like in controlling a game. The push-button switch is an input device that can be identified by its two or four legs, you can configure the Raspberry Pi program to watch out for inputs from the switch and then perform a task based on that input. This switch is only on when it is held down, unlike regular switches that latch once you switch them on until you switch them back off.

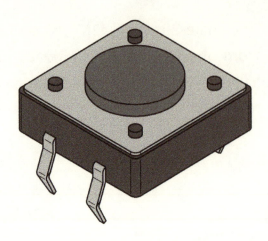

Figure 44: Push Switch

Light Emitting Diode (LED)

A light-emitting diode (LED) probably needs no introduction. It is a form of output device that emits light when current passes through it in the forward direction. It works as a transducer that is used to convert electrical energy into light. The LED is one of those low power devices that can be directly controlled from within the Raspberry Pi 4 program without the need for extra hardware. You can clearly identify them in many appliances where they are used as indicator lights or status lights for devices like a microwave, washing machine, and TVs.

Figure 45: LED Light

Resistors

Resistors restrict the flow of electrical current. The value of a resistor is measured in a unit called ohms (Ω). That means a resistor with a higher number of ohms will offer more resistance to another one with fewer ohms. One way you will use a resistor in your project will be to use it as a current limiter for the LED related projects that you have to work on. 330Ω is the typical value used for resistors in protecting LEDs.

Figure 46: Resistor

Capacitors

These are devices that store electric charges. It is measured in a unit called the Farads (F) which is the capacitance of the capacitor and a measure of the capacitor's ability to store charge.

Figure 47: Capacitor

Piezoelectric Buzzer

This is another output device also often called a buzzer or sounder. However, unlike the LED, this one produces a buzzing noise or sound as its output. The buzzer consists of a pair of metal plates within a plastic housing that vibrate against each other when active to produce the buzzing sound from the buzzer. A buzzer can either be an active buzzer or a passive buzzer, however, for our projects, it is always better to get active buzzers because they are easier to use.

Figure 48: Buzzer

Sensors

These are transducers that convert physical signals into electrical signals. They can be used in detecting movements, light, humidity and useful temperature sensors in predicting weather conditions.

Figure 49: Motion Detection

They convert sound, light, movements, proximity, touch, sights and anything humans do into electrical impulses that can now be measured and utilized by the Raspberry Pi to either make a decision or take an action.

Other useful Components for your Projects

Many other electrical components like the motor require a special kind of control board between them and the Raspberry Pi 4 when connecting them. There is quite an array of components and available equipment to be used when creating projects, chances are that any device that you conceive in your mind will already be in existence and can be bought from any shark or electrical store.

Project 4: Controlling an LED with the Raspberry Pi 4 using Scratch

This introductory project will allow you to control an LED from inside scratch using our Raspberry Pi 4.

Items Required

Hardware
- 1 qty of mini headphones or speaker
- 1 qty of 330 ohms resistor
- 4 qty of female-to-female (F2F) jumper lead
- 1 qty of LED
- Raspberry Pi 4

Software
- Raspbian
- Scratch 2

Connecting the Hardware

The LED can come in various colors, but you will notice each of them has 2 leads, one of which will be longer than the other, the longer lead is the anode and is the point that goes to the positive power supply while the shorter lead is the cathode and goes into the negative or ground of the power supply. This part with the shorter lead equally has a flattened part on the plastic part of the LED.

Now take one of the F2F jumper leads, preferably a red-colored one and connect one end to the anode (longer lead) of the LED while the other end is connected to one of the leads of the 330Ω resistor. You can also use the same color of the F2F jumper lead that you used in connecting the LED anode to continue the connection.

Now get another color of the F2F jumper lead and connect to the cathode (shorter end) of the LED leads. You should have an image like this

Figure 50: Connecting LED with Jumper Cables

Testing the LED with the Raspberry Pi 4

Remember in a previous chapter when we tried describing how the Raspberry Pi 4 works, we talked about the different pins in the GPIO. We talked about the key role you could use the 3.3V pin for was for testing the LED to be sure it is working. Now is an opportunity to use it.

You can now connect the cathode to any of the ground pins, while you connect the anode to the 3.3V pin on the GPIO of the Raspberry Pi 4, you can use the first one from the left. You can refer to the picture in figure 51.

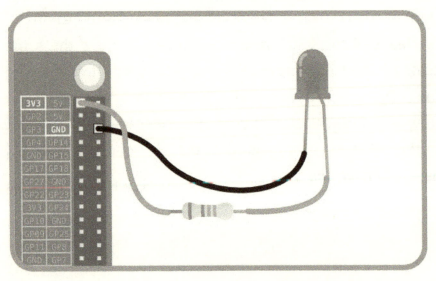

Figure 51: Testing the LED with Raspberry Pi 4

With circuit complete, you can now power the raspberry Pi 4, if everything was done correctly, the LED should come on.

Programming the LED for the Raspberry Pi 4

Now that we are confident that the LED works, we can shut down the Raspberry Pi 4 and disconnect the LED from the circuit.

It is time to write a program that will instruct the LED to turn on and off based on the instructions. Before we do that, we have to decide what output pin to use, for this project, we will be using GPIO17, one of the programmable general-purpose pins of the Raspberry Pi 4. We then connect the anode of the LED leads, the same one we connected to the 3.3V pin when testing the LED and connect it to the GPIO17 while we also connect the cathode to the ground with the jumper leads cable we used during the testing. Be careful not to short any two leads and that it is connected properly.

You can use this image as your reference.

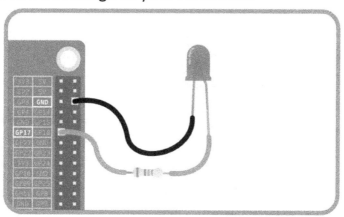

Figure 52: Connect LED to a Programmable Pin

With that concluded, let us switch on the Raspberry Pi 4 to initiate the process, once it is booted and the Raspbian OS loaded, we can now open the Scratch program by clicking the menu button (Raspberry icon at the top left), click on programming and then Scratch, we will now wait for scratch to load.

Figure 53: Selecting a New Sprite

We will not be using the cat which is the default sprite in this project, so we will right-click it and delete it. Now click the icon for new sprite under the script area to add a new sprite to the script area. You can browse around the different categories to see the options available, for our project we will use the robot from the sprites there or anyone of your choice. You can use the search button.

We will now add a trigger by clicking and dragging the "When space key is pressed" block into the script area. Next, click on the sound category and select "play sound", drag it to the script area and place it under the block we already have in the script area.

Now, your program should look like the picture in figure 54.

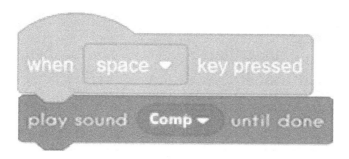

Figure 54: Play Sound with Spacebar Trigger

Now we can include the sound by clicking the robot since it is the sprite we want the sound to be added to, click the sound tab beside the costume's tab at the top of the script area and click "chose sound from library", sounds just like sprites are categorized so we will select the computer beep from the electronic category. Now click the arrow inside the "play sound" block and select the sound you just added. The robot should now have the computer beep.

Now you can test the program, remember our trigger event is no longer to click the green flag but to press the "space" button on the keyboard. If everything was done correctly, the program should run and give a beep sound.

Add the GPIO Extension to Scratch

Before we can make the scratch control the LED through the Raspberry Pi 4 GPIO's pins, we have to first enable the Pi GPIO extension to develop some extra blocks required for the interface between the Raspberry Pi 4 and Scratch.

The GPIO extension in Scratch 2 allows the program to read and control any input and output components connected to

136

the GPIO pins. You have to click "More Blocks" from the script menu among the various categories, then click the "Add an Extension" button, and double click the Pi GPIO extension to include it as one more block to choose from.

So, you can click on "more blocks" from the categories, click and drag the "set gpio to output high" and place it below the "play sound". This block is used to select specific pins on the Raspberry Pi 4's GPIO pins and set them to either high (on) or low (off) depending on what you desire to achieve with the program.

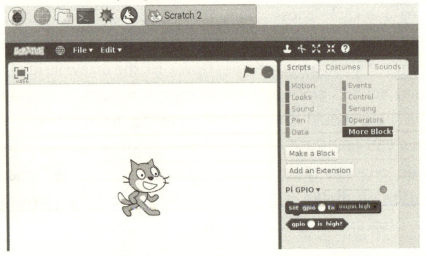

Figure 55: Adding the GPIO Pins Extension

For the pin, click the dropdown arrow and select 17 from the gpio options and leave the output option to be high. So, test the program now to see how it goes, if all goes well, the LED should light up.

Let us embellish the program a little and see what more we can add. From the control tab category, we can click the

137

block "wait for 1-sec" block and place it under the "set gpio to output high". You can change the 1 sec to 2 sec. Next, click the more block tab and drag the "set gpio to output high" to the script area. Change the pin number to 17 as we did before and change the output from high to low. This instruction will command the LED to go off after being on for 2 seconds.

You can run the program now to see how it will perform and assess the program if everything was performed correctly, there should be a computer beep played and the LED should come on and go off according to the instruction in the program.

You can save your project now.

Figure 56: Complete Project 1 Program

Project 5: Control LED with a Button Switch

Let us create a new project that will use a push button switch to put the LED on. The press switch will be used to activate the program and control the series of actions designed in the script area.

Items Required

Hardware

- 1 qty of Breadboard
- 1 qty of mini headphones or speaker
- 1 qty of 330 ohms resistor
- 4 qty of male-to-male (M2M) jumper lead
- 1 qty of male-to-female (M2F) jumper lead
- 1 qty of LED
- 1 qty of Press Switch
- Raspberry Pi 4

Software

- Raspbian OS
- Scratch 2 in which the GPIO extension has been enabled

Connecting the Hardware

Although it is possible to use our jumper leads for this project, it will be a lot easier to use a breadboard to achieve this project. The breadboard will be used to support the various components and ensure they are all connected.

The holes in a breadboard are designed to have holes apart with metallic strips under that make connections between components like a jumper lead would, only that this is a lot better and easier. It is important to understand how the metal strips that run under the holes are arranged. These holes run in rows across the board and sometimes with a gap that separates them down the middle with letters and numbers to identify them. Jumpers are useful in connecting different roles

Start by checking the type of push-button you have, if it has only two legs, ensure you put them in different tracks that do not have any connection between them, if it is a type that has four legs, you can use the middle row so that the four legs will be on four different tracks if your board can support it. Now ensure you still have the LED connected to the resistor from the previous project, if you have not, now is a good time to connect the LED using the M2F jumper lead to the 330Ω resistor, by connecting the female end to the LED and the male end to one of the tracks of the switch.

Testing the System

Test the setup by connecting the other end of the switch with the 3.3V pin on the board and the ground pin on the Raspberry Pi 4 GPIO pins to the LED as we did in the previous project. The difference this time is, for the LED to come on, you will have to press the switch and the LED will be on as long as the switch is pressed down, and it will go off when the pressed switched is released. If it works, know that you made the connection correctly, if it doesn't check your switch to ensure you place the legs where they are supposed to be and go through the connection again.

Connecting the System

If you successfully tested the connection in the previous step, you can disconnect all the jumpers from the board and the switch and run the connection based on the instruction below. Leave the switch on the breadboard as it was before.

The new connection will consist of two independent parts, the first one that connects the M2M jumper lead from the GPIO17, through the 330Ω resistor from the track on the breadboard, to the LED and to the ground pin. You can use the Gnd pin beside GPIO3. See the circuit diagram for that connection.

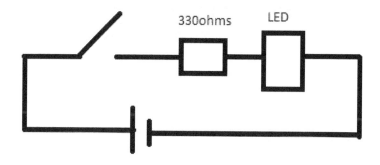

Figure 57: Circuit Diagram for LED with Switch

To achieve this on the breadboard, connect the resistor on two separate tracks, then connect the anode (longer lead) of the LED on the same track as one of the legs of the resistor, while the other legs go into a separate track. It is from this other leg of the LED that you connect it to ground on the breadboard and then using an M2M jumper lead connect the ground on the GPIO to the line on the breadboard used as the ground. The other leg of the resistor is connected to the GPIO17 equally using an M2M jumper connection to connect it to the track on which that resistor is connected. Your connection should be looking like this.

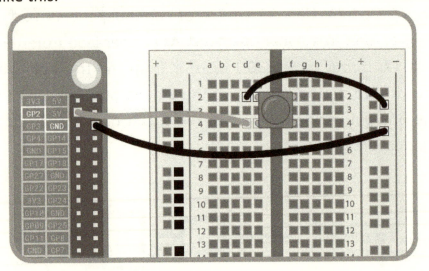

Figure 58: Install the Switch on Breadboard

The second part of the connection will be between the switch and the Raspberry Pi. You can connect the M2M lead from the GPIO2 to one of the tracks on the switch and then use another M2M jumper lead to connect the other track of the switch to the ground on the breadboard. Remember that all grounds on the Raspberry Pi 4 GPIO are common and can be used interchangeably. If done correctly, your connection should look like this.

If you know anything about electrical connections, you will immediately notice that there is no direct physical connection between the switch and the LED, instead, it is a sort of indirect connection. This connection connects the switch to the Raspberry Pi 4 to trigger it. Once triggered, the Raspberry Pi 4 program will take over the circuit from there and perform various actions based on the instruction in the program that has been set. The program can be made to make the LED stay permanently on, go on for a few minutes and then go off, come back on, etc.

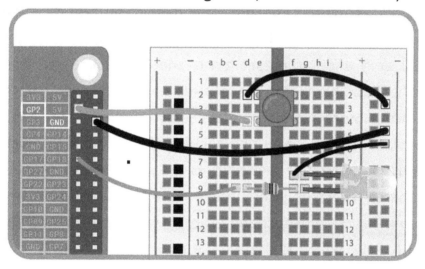

Figure 59: Control of LED with Switch

The function of the switch, in this case, will be merely to tell the scratch program that it can start executing its program rather than being a traditional switch that puts the LED on and off physically.

144

Programming Input for Pressed Switch

As in the previous section, you can now add a trigger by clicking and dragging the "When space key is pressed" block into the script area. Click and drag the "set pin to input" block and place it under the "when space key is pressed" block in the script area. Now select the gpio2 pin you connected the switch to in the GPIO pins, then change the "output" to "input" to configure the pin as an input pin rather than the default output pin.

Now let us extend the program further by adding other blocks. We will start by adding the forever block to the script area under the "set pin to input" block. Next, drag the "if-then" block and place it inside the "forever" block. From the More blocks 'palette, select "Pio is high?" block and place it in the diamond section of the "if then" block. The diamond part of that block is the point where data are compared which is later used to make a decision. In the "gpio is high?" block, change the pin number to 2 and the high to low, which is the pin we connected our switch to, which tells the program which pin to check to know if it is low.

Remember that the pins are high by default, so when the switch is pressed, it becomes low and so triggers the program.

Next, we want to direct the program on what to do when it receives a signal that the button has been pressed. To perform that, let us click and drag the "say Hello! For 2 sec" to the script area under the "gpio is low" and change the "Hello!" to, "You just pressed a button".

Next, we can decide to include a sound to be played when the button is pressed by dragging the "play sound" block directly under the "You just pressed a button" block we just edited. We then select the sound we want to be played by clicking the robot sprite we have in the script area, click the sound tab beside the script tab at the top and click "chose sound from library", select the computer beep or any other sound from the any of the categories as we did before. Now click the arrow inside the "play sound" block in the script area and select the sound you just added. The robot should now have the computer beep or whatever sound you added.

When we run the program, that should be what appears on the screen and the sound we will hear.

At the same time as that is running, we also want the LED to come on, to achieve that, we will add another block, "set gpio to output high" block to the script area and place it under the "play sound" block we just added all under the forever block. We will then change the pin number to 17 and leave the output as high.

We can now test the system. If everything goes well, there will be a display on the screen, a computer beep sound and the LED comes on.

You can save your project now.

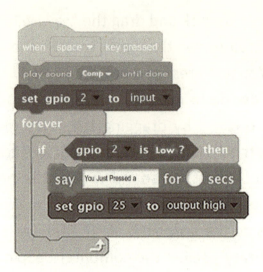

Figure 60: Complete Project 2 Program

Project 6: Astable Multivibrator

Astable multivibrators are very useful in pulse storing, generating, and counting circuits. They are simple types of two-stage circuits also called a relaxation circuit in which the circuit oscillates between two quasi-stable (half-stable) states and continues in that oscillating state until it has to be stopped.

In an astable multivibrator, when one of the states is high, the other goes low, the same way, when that other state goes high, the initial state goes low and vice versa.

They are valuable in engineering as standard frequency sources, useful in radar and TV circuits and also as memory elements in computer systems.

147

In this project, we will have two LEDs instead of one as in the previous project, then we will set it up such that once the system is triggered when the switch is pressed, the first LED will come on while the other is off, then the second LED will come on while the first one will now go off.

Items Required

Hardware

- 1 qty of Breadboard
- 1 qty of mini headphones or speaker
- 2 qty of 330 ohms resistor
- 6 qty of male-to-male (M2M) jumper lead
- 1 qty of male-to-female (M2F) jumper lead
- 2 qty of LED
- 1 qty of Press Switch
- Raspberry Pi 4

Software

- Raspbian OS
- Scratch 2 in which the GPIO extension has been enabled

Testing the New Component

To test the new resistor and LED, we intend to use in this project, we can refer to project 1 and use the same testing method to ensure the LED is working.

Setting up the Hardware

For this project, we will use the same setup as the previous setup in project 2, we will merely add a few more components to it to extend the functionality of that project to achieve our astable multivibrator.

If you did not set up the hardware of the previous project (project 2) or have already disconnected it, you have to go back to set up the hardware and the software before you can come to this stage of the project.

To extend the project, we only have to make a slight physical modification on the board by adding another 330Ω resistor to the breadboard on a separate track similar to the way we did the previous one, then we connect the anode of the LED from the same track as one end of the resistor leads and connect the other end of the LED to a new track.

We can then connect the cathode of the LED to the ground on the GPIO's pins of the Raspberry Pi 4 using an M2M jumper lead and connect the other end of the resistor track to the pin on the Raspberry Pi 4 labeled GPIO22. Now the hardware is complete.

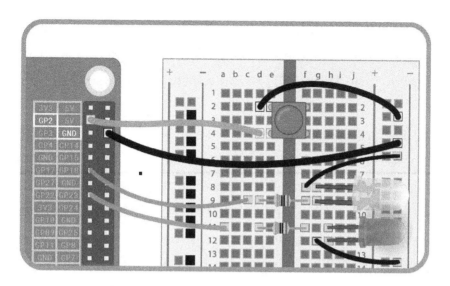

Figure 61: Astable Multivibrator Connection on Breadboard

Programming the Raspberry Pi 4 as an Astable Multivibrator

Once again as in the preceding section, you start by adding a trigger by clicking and dragging the "When space key is pressed" block into the script area. Next, click and drag the "set gpio to output high" block and place it under the "when space key is pressed" block in the script area. Now select the gpio2 on the block since it is the pin you connected the switch to in the Raspberry Pi 4's GPIO pins, then change the "output" to "input" to configure the pin as an input pin rather than its default output pin.

Next, drag the "forever" block and place it under the "set pin to input" block. From the More blocks' palette, select "set gpio to output high" block and put it in the forever

150

block. In the "set gpio to output high" block, change the pin number to 17 which will direct the program to switch to whatever is on the GPIO17 lead which in our case is the LED light.

Next, we will drag the "wait 1 sec" block to the program and place it under the "set gpio to output high" block and change the time from 1 to 2 seconds. Drag another "set gpio to output high" block to the script area under the "wait 2 sec" block and change the pin number to 17 and output to low. By setting the pin to an output low, it will switch off the LED connected to that circuit. Add another "wait 1 sec" block to the program and place it under the "set gpio 17 to output low" and change it to 2 seconds.

Again, drag the "set gpio to output high" block and place it under the one we just added and change the pin number to 22 which will tell the program to switch on whatever is on the GPIO2 lead which in our case is the second LED light.

Next, we will again drag the "wait 1 sec" block to the program and place it under the "set gpio 22 to output high" block and alter the time from 1 sec to 2 seconds. Then you drag another "set gpio to output high" block to the script area under the "wait 2 sec" block and change the pin number to 22 and output to low. Again, changing the output to low will switch off the LED after 2 seconds. Place another "wait 1 sec" block to the program and place it under the "set gpio 22 to output low" and change the time to 2 seconds.

Now test the program by clicking the trigger button which for our project is the space bar, if you did it correctly, then the first LED will come on for 2 seconds, after which it will go off and then the second LED will come on for 2 seconds, after which it will go off and then the first LED will come on again and the process will continue until you stop it.

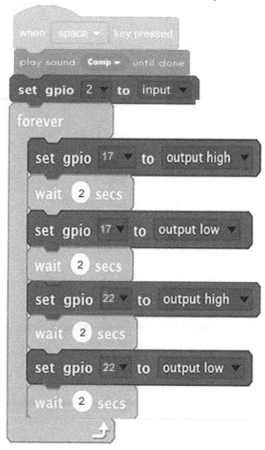

Figure 62: Complete Project 3 Program

You can now save your project under the file's menu.

Now, the program should look like figure 62. We can now test the system. If everything goes well, there will be a display on the screen, a computer beep sound and the two LEDs coming on and off alternately.

If you have any previous experience with electronics and having to connect various components together to achieve what we just did, then you will appreciate the enormous power of the Raspberry pi and how it simplifies the building of circuit compared to if this same project was built using transistors, capacitors, and resistors.

The picture in figure 63 is the circuit of an astable multivibrator achieved by using discrete components. Now, compare this with using a program to achieve the same output and how we were able to upgrade our initial project 5 so easily into project 6. You will agree that the Raspberry Pi makes life a lot easier.

Figure 63: Astable Multivibrator with Discrete Electronic Components

Assignment

1: Extend this project such that when the switch is operated a second time, the whole program stops. (Hint: Use variables to store values.)

Appendix

Raspberry Pi 1 Model A+ 512MB: Technical Specifications

700 MHz ARM11 processor

512 MB RAM

Four-pole 3.5 mm jack with audio output and composite video output

Camera interface (CSI)

Micro SD card slot

One USB port

Display interface (DSI)

40-pin GPIO header with 0.1"-spaced male pins

Full-size HDMI output

Raspberry Pi 1 Model B: Technical Specifications

Broadcom BCM2835

700 MHz single-core ARM

256 MB later 512 MB

Slot for SD Card

3.5 mm jack or via HDMI

Composite & HDMI

Broadcom VideoCore IV @ 250 MHz

2 USB Ports

85 mm x 56 mm

5V ~600-800 ma

1 Ethernet port 10/100 RJ45 jack

26 pins GPIO

Raspberry Pi 2 Model B 1GB: Technical Specifications

Broadcom BCM2837 Arm7 Quad Core Processor powered Single Board Computer running at 900MHz

1GB RAM

4 x USB 2 ports

4 pole Stereo output and Composite video port

CSI camera port for connecting the Raspberry Pi camera

40 pins extended GPIO

Full-size HDMI

Micro USB power source

DSI display port for connecting the Raspberry Pi touch screen display

Micro SD port for loading your operating system and storing data

Raspberry Pi 3 Model B+: Technical Specifications

1.4GHz 64-bit quad-core ARM Cortex-A53 CPU (BCM2837)

1GB RAM (LPDDR2 SDRAM)

Camera interface (CSI)

Display interface (DSI)

4 x USB 2.0 ports

On-board wireless LAN - dual-band 802.11 b/g/n/ac

microSD slot

40 GPIO pins

Full-size HDMI 1.3a port

On-board Bluetooth 4.2 HS low-energy

Combined 3.5mm analog audio and composite video jack

300 Mbit/s ethernet

Video Core IV multimedia/3D graphics core @ 400MHz/300MHz

Raspberry Pi 3 Model B: Technical Specification

Broadcom BCM2387 chipset

1.2GHz Quad-Core ARM Cortex-A53

802.11 bgn Wireless LAN and Bluetooth 4.1 (Bluetooth Classic and LE)

1GB RAM

64 Bit CPU

DSI display port for connecting the Raspberry Pi touch screen display

CSI camera port for connecting the Raspberry Pi camera

Micro USB power source

Micro SD port for loading your operating system and storing data

Full-size HDMI

4 x USB ports

4 pole Stereo output and Composite video port

10/100 BaseT Ethernet socket

Cortex-A53: Technical Specification

ARM ISA: ARMv8 (32/64-bit)

Integer Mul: 1

Integer Add: 2

Load/Store Units: 1

Branch Units: 1

FP/NEON ALUs: 1x64-bit

Issue Width: 2 micro-ops

Pipeline Length: 8

L1 Cache: 8KB-64KB I$ + 8KB-64KB D$

L2 Cache: 128KB - 2MB (Optional)

ARM Cortex-A72 processor: Technical Specification

Produced   2016
Predecessor ARM Cortex-A57
Microarchitecture ARMv8-A
Successor   ARM Cortex-A73
Cores 1–4 per cluster, multiple clusters
Min. feature size   16 nm
L1 cache   80 KiB (48 KiB I-cache with parity, 32 KiB D-cache with ECC) per core
L2 cache   512 KiB to 4 MiB
L3 cache   None

www.ingramcontent.com/pod-product-compliance
Lightning Source LLC
Chambersburg PA
CBHW051053050326
40690CB00006B/702